The Beatitudes

Ronald Lello divides his time between supporting the Millennium Trust, a forum for seekers of truth in London, originating religious documentaries and restoring his historic house and garden in Kent, England. His work for television includes *Revelations,* which ran for five years, a five-part series on the Gnostics, and the current series, *Blessed are they ...* He has published *Revelations: Glimpses of Reality* about profound spiritual experience of the soul in an age of sceptical scientific materialism.

The Beatitudes

Living with Blessings, Meditation and Prayer

Ronald Lello

ELEMENT

Shaftesbury, Dorset ● Rockport, Massachusetts
Melbourne, Victoria

© Element Books Limited 1997
Text © Ronald Lello 1997

First published in Great Britain in 1997 by
Element Books Limited
Shaftesbury, Dorset SP7 8BP

Published in the USA in 1997 by
Element Books, Inc.
PO Box 830, Rockport, MA 01966

Published in Australia in 1997 by
Element Books and distributed
by Penguin Books Australia Ltd
487 Maroondah Highway, Ringwood,
Victoria 3134

Cover design by Mark Slader
Designed and typeset by
Linda Reed and Associates
Printed and bound in the USA
by Courier Westford Inc., MA.

British Library Cataloguing in Publication
data available

Library of Congress Cataloging in Publication
data available

ISBN 1 86204 154 7

Contents

Acknowledgements   ix
Foreword by Kathleen Raine   xi
Introduction   xiii

ॐ THE BEATITUDES ॐ

The Poor in Spirit   3
They that Mourn   23
The Meek   37
Hunger and Thirst   53
The Merciful   69
The Pure in Heart   85
The Peacemakers   97
The Persecuted   111

Epilogue   123
Reflection and Meditation   129
Bibliography   133
Meditation Centres   135
Index of First Lines   136

To Sheila

A true Pythagorean, a Lady
and a beloved friend of many

ACKNOWLEDGEMENTS

So many people bring an influence to the writing of a book, but whereas I have difficulty about who not to include, I have no problem in deciding where to begin. I am deeply indebted to Sir Kenneth Jupp for his great and generous help, encouragement and guidance whenever I asked for it. Then I must thank Fred Proud and Elizabeth Best for being present at a difficult birth and to Eric Robson for suggesting the conception! Mira Shapiro and Warren Kenton, Revd David Hancock, Joan Crammond, Sister Edmée Kingsmill slg, and Nathan Rabin all took so much trouble to answer questions, and to Cheryl Howeld for her illustrations. To Kathleen Raine goes gratitude for always being there at both good and difficult times, and for her Foreword. Gratitude also goes to Kapila Vatsyayan who, with a single word, changed a man's life, and to the author of *Satsang* whose words live to illuminate! Border Television and its Chairman, James Graham, are much deserving of praise for their continued support of the spiritual quest; also the *Blessed are they …* production team and all those we interviewed – everyone played their part. Finally, to my wife Angela who has suffered much during these past weeks, and to Florence Hamilton and Matthew Cory, my editors, who have suffered even more. To all of you, and others too, I say, 'Don't stop here – keep peeling the onion!'

The publishers would like to acknowledge the use of extracts from the following: the *Authorized Version* of the Bible (The King James Bible), the rights of which are vested in the Crown, reproduced by permission of the Crown's Patentee, Cambridge University Press, Cambridge, UK; *New Jerusalem Bible*, copyright 1985, reproduced by permission of Doubleday, a division of Bantam Doubleday Dell Publishing Group Inc. and Darton, Longman & Todd Ltd; *Daily Study Bible*, reproduced by permission of Saint Andrew Press, Edinburgh; *The Message Bible*, reproduced by permission of NavPress Publishing Group, Colorado Springs; Scripture quotations where indicated are from the *Contemporary English Version*© American Bible Society 1991, 1992, 1995, used by permission; *Prayers of the Cosmos*, reproduced by permission of HarperCollins Publishers Inc., New York.

Foreword

The 'sayings' of the great world-teachers, being words of the most profound wisdom, one might expect to be understood only by exceptionally intelligent or learned people, or by initiates of some esoteric group. On the contrary, the words of Krishna, Moses, Jesus and the prophet Mohammed were addressed to unlettered men and women and have since been heard and understood by generations of humankind. For wisdom is not 'difficult' and is the more profound as it speaks immediately to all.

Modern education tends to teach us 'about' (Plato or Shakespeare or the Gospels or whatever it may be) whereas we should be learning 'from'. Ronald Lello is not giving us information, or proposing a theory about the Beatitudes but presenting them as they would have been understood within the context of the time and place of Jesus' Sermon on the Mount, and as they can be applied in our own time. The Beatitudes themselves were not new: all of them belong to the traditional wisdom of the Jewish people. Jesus took themes, and often words, from the Hebrew scriptures, already familiar to his hearers, and, until recently, no less familiar to us through the Christian Gospels. There is nothing novel about the great truths by which humanity lives, for we do not live by 'bread alone' but by 'every word of God', common to all sacred traditions because grounded in reality itself.

Ronald Lello writes as a man committed to the truths he presents, in a way that the Everyman of today cannot fail to understand. He uses a number of translations, including the King James Authorized Version and the Catholic *New Jerusalem Bible*, but also less familiar versions calculated to make us see the familiar in a new light, sometimes, indeed, to shock us into radical revisioning. Above all, he makes clear that these teachings are not instructions for private reflections, but for the proper conduct of human relationships in a closely knit society. Much that is now deemed the domain of the 'science of economics' proves to be a question of human behaviour and the responsibility required of individuals towards one another. Jesus was expounding the laws of his 'Kingdom of Heaven', which is the human kingdom itself, here and now, in this world, for those who choose to live by its simple rules of 'mercy, pity, peace, love', be we 'heathen, Turk or Jew' or indeed practising Christians.

Kathleen Raine

Introduction

There are certain conversations I have had at odd moments in my life which I have never forgotten. I was once lost without a map in the leafy county of Surrey. Eventually the road took me to a village where I encountered an Old Man seated on a wooden chair under the shade of a huge tree. I stopped and asked him for directions. They took some time in coming because first he wanted to talk about everything under the sun. Several things he said have remained in my memory. It is interesting what the mind retains with such clarity and what is dismally forgotten.

He spoke about Bible study and said that if you want to understand anything in the Bible you should take a word and look up every reference you can find for it. Each time a reference is found it should be held in the mind until the mind gently rests on it. Once this happens it is time to let go and move on to the next word. He said if this was done properly the way would be known and people wouldn't have to trouble others for directions. He might have been a wise man. The few I have met have always related what happens in ordinary life to what goes on in the spiritual world.

Anyway, a little later I tried out what he told me to do and found it to be impossible. My mind kept thinking about anything but the word and the sentences I wanted to understand. So I forgot all about it – except whenever I heard the Bible being read, back came the Old Man's advice. Many years later on a train journey with Eric Robson, the presenter of Border Television's network series, *Blessed are they ...*, we began to discuss the possibility of writing a book about the Beatitudes. I decided to try the exercise again.

I cannot say I have found it any easier to hold a word or an idea gently in mind. Many will recognize this exercise as an ancient spiritual discipline called 'reflection'. Guidance on how it can be perfected is to be found in a number of books on the subject. It is based on the premise that understanding is not conditional upon logic or rationality alone. Rational thought is just one way to understand. Another is to let the mind dwell on a theme. At first the mind presents all manner of things which have nothing to do with what is being considered. But a combination of patience and persistence may sometimes yield surprising results and a new and fresh understanding may be brought into being. This method seems able to transcend the mundane processes of rationality. Armed with it, albeit imperfectly practised, and with Bibles and a copy of

Cruden's Concordance, the research for this book was begun without much idea of where it would lead.

It is hoped that readers will also equip themselves with Bibles and concordances and practise this exercise. There are many different views about what the Beatitudes mean and some of them appear to conflict with others. One of the purposes of this book is to encourage readers to seek out understandings for themselves. In the United Kingdom, the book accompanies a television series about the Beatitudes in which people find themselves in situations where they meet the challenges presented by these sayings. What emerged from the preparation of the series was that the Beatitudes represent something very individual and special, not just to those being interviewed but also to those who were helping produce the programmes. Living with the texts over many months, I found they mirrored aspects of my life I needed to know about.

So it seemed wrong to write a generalized account of what the Beatitudes mean. This is not to suggest that a true meaning does not exist. We may approach the truth by different routes, therefore, what we understand while journeying will vary. If we hold onto something we have understood at some time in the past, our journey comes to a halt. We all need to remember that knowledge changes as understanding deepens. This book is the account of one journey. If the journey were to be taken again, I would expect the result to be different. If this journey is of interest, it may raise some questions and inspire readers to set out on their own explorations.

The translations of the Beatitudes vary considerably. As a preface to each chapter I have selected six ways of formulating them to demonstrate this range. Of these I confess to having a warm regard for the American Bible, *The Message*, translated by Eugene H Peterson. In that special way in which Americans can use the English language, he so often manages to catch a meaning in just a few words and gives new life to it. His translation of the first Beatitude is a classic. I have also included a translation by Neil Douglas-Klotz, *Prayers of the Cosmos*. He has attempted to rediscover the Aramaic, which many believe was the language Jesus would have used most frequently. I cannot say I agree with his view but I do applaud the way he has established a system of prayer and meditation and breathing exercises which are essential to his approach.

The quotations selected to illuminate the main text have come from two Bibles: the Protestant Authorized Version of King James, 1611, and the Standard Edition of the Catholic *New Jerusalem Bible* published in English in 1985. (These are denoted in text by the letters *AV* and *J* respectively.) The King James Bible offers some of the most beautiful examples of the English language and its poetry often conveys a meaning far beyond its words. But it can be misleading and in places incorrect, so it is useful to have some modern scholarship available. Of the modern versions, I selected the *New*

Jerusalem Bible partly because it retains a poetic style and, even more importantly, its notes on the text are clear and very informative. I was suprised to find that although the Beatitudes are frequently referred to, few books have been written about them. Of those available *Spirituality of the Beatitudes* by Michael H Crosby is excellent and deals with many issues beyond the scope of this book. For more general reading, William Barclay's *Daily Study Bible* on the Gospel of St Matthew must be highly recommended. His wordy version of each Beatitude quoted in this book is not at all typical of his clear and easy style and he has wonderful stories.

For those interested in the philosophic issues which may be raised in this book, Ananda Coomaraswamy's essays on metaphysics are essential reading. His is the tradition of 'non-dualism' or Advaita philosophy, and one of the great gifts he offers this age, one in which religion continues to viciously divide humankind, is to demonstrate the unific nature of wisdom. Just as this text was going to the printers I was given a book, *Grace and Mortgage* by Peter Selby, Bishop of Worcester. It looks to be highly relevant to questions raised in the chapter on The Merciful, and must-be worth purchasing for the bibliography alone.

The Beatitudes form the introduction according to St Matthew to the Sermon on the Mount (Matthew 5), the essence of the Christian way. They are quoted in part in St Luke (Luke 6), who has the best version of the 'maledictions', those 'woe unto him' passages in which

Jesus promises the direst of fates for hypocrites and evil doers. But St Matthew organizes the Beatitudes to herald the Sermon. We cannot know exactly how Jesus spoke these sayings. St Matthew's treatment of them may well have met the specific needs of his own time and place, something many modern Christians find unacceptable due to a slavish adherence to historical authenticity.

What is clear is that the Beatitudes given by Jesus have the mark of the divine teacher. They are brief, simple and profound. They inspire insight and art, and evoke curiosity about things familiar but not quite seen. From them has come great music, from that of the fifth-century divine, St John Chrysostom, to the soul-searching cadences of John Tavener. They have been a source of strength and comfort and have brought illumination to countless Christians and those of other faiths. Buddhists, Hindus, masters of Vedanta, philosophers and esotericists have discovered something in the Beatitudes of universal appeal. Something in these aphorisms sits easily in all religious traditions, yet what creates this universal response is beyond definition or analysis.

It may have something to do with the word common to all the Beatitudes – 'blessed'. This word has a beautiful sound. It has warmth and simplicity. In English, the word has always meant something special, usually something divine. Psalm 41 not only shows this, but is perhaps the inspiration for the first Beatitude:

Blessed is he that considereth the poor: the Lord will
deliver him in time of trouble.

The Lord will preserve him, and keep him alive; and
he shall be blessed upon the earth: and thou wilt not
deliver him unto the will of his enemies.

PSALM 41 *AV*

The Greek word which St Matthew uses means 'happy'.
It is not a word which promises to confer something in
the future. It describes a *present* state of being: 'Happy
are the Poor in Spirit.' This hardly has the same effect
upon the ear and provokes the question raised later,
how can someone be happy while they are in mourning? 'Blessed' implies something more permanent than
our modern idea of happiness. Perhaps 'joy' conveys
something of what Jesus and St Matthew intended. But
the only way really to know what is meant is to keep
one of them in mind each day and put it into practice.

The Poet Laureate Ted Hughes prefaced a copy of his
anthology *The Essential Shakespeare* with the words: 'If
one passage is learned every morning, the character will
improve even if the memory does not!'

Good advice which we would do well to apply to
biblical texts.

The Beatitudes

CHAPTER *1*

The Poor in Spirit

Blessed are the poor in spirit:
for theirs is the kingdom of heaven.
AUTHORIZED VERSION

How blessed are the poor in spirit:
the kingdom of Heaven is theirs.
NEW JERUSALEM BIBLE

O the bliss of the man who has realised
his own utter helplessness and who has put
his whole trust in God,
For thus alone he can render to God that perfect
obedience which will make him
a citizen of the kingdom of Heaven.
DAILY STUDY BIBLE

You're blessed when you're at the end of your rope.
With less of you there is more of God and his rule.
THE MESSAGE

God blesses those people who depend only on him.
They belong to the kingdom of heaven!
CONTEMPORARY ENGLISH VERSION

Happy and aligned with the One are those who
find their home in the breathing;
to them belong the inner kingdom and queendom
of heaven.
PRAYERS OF THE COSMOS

*E*veryone is looking for certainty. Even the scientists who develop theories about uncertainty in the universe want to be certain about what they say. It does seem that we humans are happier when we feel secure and confident. So when an idea comes along which creates uncertainty, we either ignore it or turn it into something else.

Poverty is such an idea. People say poverty is a source of unhappiness. Many think it is a cause of crime.

Some preachers and clergymen encourage people to pray fervently to God for money and wealth so as to free themselves from 'the pit of sin' which they say poverty creates. We are all certain that poverty is bad news, especially the imminent prospect of our own poverty.

So this first Beatitude comes as a shock. Its impact is to jeopardize an idea about which we are certain. In this saying of Jesus, we encounter an idea which threatens the secure economic basis of our family, our society and our culture.

There are two versions of the Beatitude. The Gospeller Luke is uncompromising:

> Blessed be ye poor: for yours is the kingdom of God.
>
> LUKE 6 *AV*

Matthew is different. He qualifies 'the poor' by writing:

> Blessed are the poor in spirit: for theirs is the kingdom of heaven.
>
> MATTHEW 5 *AV*

It is the addition of 'in spirit' which helps wealthy people and those who want to be wealthy to feel better. It may account for the line taken by many Bible commentators who suggest that the Beatitude emphasizes spiritual rather than material poverty. Does this Beatitude really mean poor people, and just how poor do you have to be to qualify?

Luke reported Jesus as saying:

> How hard it is for those who have riches to make their way into the kingdom of God! Yes, it is easier for a camel to pass through the eye of a needle than for someone rich to enter the kingdom of God.

LUKE 18 *J*

And then, perhaps, some well-fed and comfortable people asked nervously:

> In that case, who can be saved?

Jesus replied enigmatically:

> Things that are impossible by human resources, are possible for God.

LUKE 18 *J*

This next story raises the question of the relationship between riches and greed:

> There was a rich man who used to dress in purple and fine linen and feast magnificently every day. And at his gate there used to lie a poor man called Lazarus, covered in sores, who longed to fill himself with what fell from the rich man's table. Even dogs came and licked his sores. Now it happened that the poor man died and was carried away by the angels into Abraham's embrace. The rich man also died and was buried.
>
> In his torment in Hades he looked up and saw Abraham a long way off with Lazarus in his embrace. So he cried out, 'Father Abraham, pity me and send Lazarus to dip the tip of his finger in water and cool

my tongue, for I am in agony in these flames.' Abraham said, 'My son, remember that during your life you had your fill of good things, just as Lazarus had his fill of bad. Now he is comforted here while you are in agony. But that is not all: between us and you a great gulf has been fixed, to prevent those who want to cross from our side to yours or from your side to ours.'

So he said, 'Father, I beg you then to send Lazarus to my father's house, since I have five brothers, to give them warning so that they do not come to this place of torment too.' Abraham said, 'They have Moses and the prophets, let them listen to them.' The rich man replied, 'Ah no, Father Abraham, but if someone comes to them from the dead they will repent.' Then Abraham said to him, 'If they will not listen to Moses or to the prophets, they will not be convinced even if someone should rise from the dead.'

LUKE 16 J

Perhaps this is why Proverbs maintains:

Better someone poor living an honest life,
than someone of devious ways however rich.

PROVERBS 28 J

In the story the 'rich man' didn't seem to be all bad. Once he realized his mistake he did try to warn his brothers. Yet this good impulse wasn't enough to save him or his brothers. In this and other sayings and parables Jesus held that being rich is an impediment to entering the kingdom of heaven.

At the time the Gospellers were writing, three different Greek words were used to translate the same Hebrew word for 'poor'. The Greek word in this particular Beatitude was the one used to describe economic poverty. It was used twice in St Matthew: in this Beatitude, and to describe Lazarus, the beggar at the gate who was covered in sores and licked by dogs. If Matthew's Greek was accurate, Jesus was referring specifically to beggars, people whose material and physical poverty was of the worst kind

Yet can Jesus really have been speaking of physical poverty? Many biblical scholars believe that these stories are not to be taken literally. For them, they are allegories about the 'inner state of our being' or about the state of our soul. Typical of these writers is William Barclay, who points out:

> We must be careful not to think that this Beatitude calls actual material poverty a good thing ... Jesus would never have called blessed a state where people live in slums and have not enough to eat ... That kind of poverty it is the aim of Christianity to remove. The poverty which is blessed is the poverty of spirit ...
>
> DAILY STUDY BIBLE

It would be difficult to argue against the idea that one of the aims of Christianity is to alleviate poverty. But the possibility that spiritual poverty will lead to material poverty is not considered, for Jesus has said that the poor in spirit are blessed. A direct connection between the two conditions is unthinkable to the Christian mind. Yet in his letter to the Corinthians, we have a clear indication of how St Paul was living his Christianity:

> Here we are, fools for Christ's sake, while you are the clever ones in Christ; we are weak, while you are strong; you are honoured, while we are disgraced. To this day we go short of food and drink and clothes, we are beaten up and we have no homes; we earn our living by labouring with our own hands; when we are cursed, we answer with a blessing; when we are hounded, we endure it passively; when we are insulted, we give a courteous answer. We are treated even now as the dregs of the world, the very lowest scum.
>
> 1 CORINTHIANS 4 *J*

Within a few years of Jesus' teaching, there was already dissension between rich and poor in the church. We need to know more about spiritual poverty and how to recognize it. In the absence of clear examples being given by Jesus, it is in the Old Testament that we find descriptions of those times when we are at our weakest, times when life seems too much to bear.

There is no shortage of this kind of writing in the Old Testament. The history of the Jewish people is inextricably linked with collective and personal suffering. Many of us will have experienced the emotional darkness of these poems at some time in our lives:

Save me, God, for the waters
 have closed in on my very being.
I am sinking in the deepest swamp
 and there is no firm ground.
I have stepped into deep water
 and the waves are washing over me.
I am exhausted with calling out, my throat is hoarse,
 my eyes are worn out with searching for my God.

PSALM 69 *J*

When I call, answer me, God, upholder of my right.
In my distress you have set me at large;
 take pity on me and hear my prayer!

PSALM 4 *J*

My God, my God, why have you forsaken me?
The words of my groaning do nothing to save me.
My God, I call by day but you do not answer,
 at night, but I find no respite.

PSALM 22 *J*

These moments described by the poets are terrible to bear. We seem to have done everything in our power to change our situation yet still our world continues to collapse about us. At such times we may well implore, 'Dear God, if you are really there, please, please change this situation', and yet the suffering continues. Being 'at the end of your rope' is an apt description. But who can be full of joy or experience a state of supreme happiness, while tearing their heart out, sobbing into a pillow? One state may follow the other, but to experience both at the same time ... ? The Beatitude says 'Blessed are ...' not 'Blessed will be ...'!

The Greek word for 'spirit' used by Matthew can mean wind, breath, life, even soul. The words soul and spirit are interchanged without warning by Christians, and people have used them over the centuries to mean different things and sometimes the same thing. It has been suggested the word spirit describes that part of us which is closest to God and which shares in His being. It is like the soul of the soul. It is the divine spark in us. Therefore it is difficult to understand how such a thing could be called rich or poor.

Being poor or being rich is to do with the means to sustain life. Being rich means having an abundance of things. Rich land has an abundance of qualities necessary to produce great harvests. When we speak of poor land, we mean land which is lacking in the nutrients to feed and sustain plants. A rich person has far more than is needed to sustain life. A poor person is dependent upon others.

If we were to speak of our soul being poor, it might mean we lack strength of will or purpose, rather as in the psalms we were quoting. But whose will is being referred to here – 'my will' or 'God's will'? Eugene Peterson's version of the first Beatitude in *The Message* Bible rightly says 'with less of you there is more of God'. One way of understanding the soul is to see it as a mirror. It reflects the divine light of the spirit, as well as the darker light of the mind and the bodily senses. Both worlds are reflected in the mirror. Our problem is that our mirrors are covered in grime. Just occasionally it is as if they are wiped clean and we glimpse the divine light. Then, we instantaneously become conscious of truth and happiness. It all happens in a moment. Our minds are transformed. Everything we experience is beautiful. And then it has gone!

But if our spirit is the divine light within us, how could that ever be thought of as rich or poor? The divine sustains everything. It is God in us. If it fails to provide the nutrients we need for life, where else or to whom else can Christians turn? The misuse of such important words like soul and spirit creates confusion. Take Psalm 6 in which the poet expresses a feeling of weakness in body and being. First, here is the Authorized Version:

> O Lord heal me; for my bones are vexed.
> My soul is also sore vexed …

On this reading it suggests that the psalmist is physically exhausted and emotionally drained. Yet something is still watching to remind him that God is present. And now the *New Jerusalem Bible*, a modern translation which uses 'spirit' instead of 'soul':

> Heal me, Yahweh, my bones are shaken,
> my spirit is shaken to its very depths …

So what is it in the psalmist that knows the spirit is shaken to its depths? Something in him is disturbed.

But is it the divine spark, the divine presence in him, or is it his memories, ideas and emotions which are troubled yet being watched by the spirit?

Here is the whole psalm in the Authorized Version:

O Lord, rebuke me not in thine anger, neither
chasten me in thy hot displeasure.

Have mercy upon me, O Lord; for I am weak:
O Lord, heal me; for my bones are vexed.

My soul is also sore vexed: but thou, O Lord,
how long?

Return, O Lord, deliver my soul: oh save me for thy
mercies' sake.

For in death there is no remembrance of thee: in the
grave who shall give thee thanks?

I am weary with my groaning; all the night make I
my bed to swim; I water my couch with my tears.

Mine eye is consumed because of grief; it waxeth old
because of all mine enemies.

Depart from me, all ye workers of iniquity; for the
Lord hath heard the voice of my weeping.

The Lord hath heard my supplication; the Lord will
receive my prayer.

Let all mine enemies be ashamed and sore vexed: let
them return and be ashamed suddenly.

PSALM 6 *AV*

What is left after death must be that in us which is not subject to death. Not the body, perhaps not the mind, but of certainty that which cannot die is spirit. And if the spirit is not subject to death, is it likely to become rich or poor? Even so, the meaning of 'poor in spirit' is elusive.

Would the promise which follows 'for theirs is the kingdom of heaven' throw some light on the problem? What is this 'kingdom'? The best-known reference comes in the prayer he gave for all to use – The Lord's Prayer:

> Our Father in heaven,
> may your name be held holy,
> your kingdom come
> your will be done,
> on earth as in heaven.
> Give us today our daily bread.
> And forgive us our debts,
> as we have forgiven those who are in debt to us.
> And do not put us to the test,
> but save us from the Evil One.
>
> MATTHEW 6 J

The word 'kingdom' has come to mean the land which belongs to a king or a nation state (as in the United Kingdom). But when the Bible was first translated into the English language, the word kingdom carried the meaning 'the rule of' or 'the law of', so that the words 'thy kingdom come' or 'your kingdom come' did not mean a physical place where God would be encountered at some future point in time. It meant a condition or a system where God's law prevailed. When a group of Jews who strictly followed the Old Testament law asked Jesus when this rule was to come he replied:

> The coming of the kingdom of God does not admit of observation and there will be no one to say 'Look it is here! Look it is there!' For look, the kingdom of God is among you.
>
> LUKE 17 J

The scholars say he meant that the kingdom is already present here and now for those who can see it. 'For look, the kingdom of God is among you.' This means that the kingdom of heaven is the rule which is to be 'done on earth'. Interestingly enough the word 'earth' in Hebrew also means 'land', something we shall be looking at in the third Beatitude. On another occasion the disciples asked Jesus why he spoke to people in story form. In his reply Jesus said there were two groups of people; those who understood his words and those who didn't:

> Then the disciples went up to him and asked, 'Why do you talk to them in parables?' In answer, he said, 'Because to you is granted to understand the mysteries of the kingdom of Heaven, but to them it is not granted. Anyone who has, will be given more and will have more than enough; but anyone who has not will be deprived even of what he has. The reason I talk to them

in parables is that they look without seeing and listen without hearing or understanding. So in their case what was spoken by the prophet Isaiah is being fulfilled:

Listen and listen, but never understand!
Look and look, but never perceive!
This people's heart has grown coarse,
their ears dulled, they have shut their eyes tight
to avoid using their eyes to see, their ears to hear,
their heart to understand, changing their ways
and being healed by me.

But blessed are your eyes because they see, your ears because they hear! In truth I tell you, many prophets and upright people longed to see what you see, and never saw it; to hear what you hear, and never heard it.

MATTHEW 13 *J*

We are always wanting to be somewhere else, moving on to the next thing or thinking about something other than what is in front of us. We worry about the past or the future and rarely are content with the present. Stress increasingly affects all of us and has much to do with worrying about what happened yesterday or what will happen tomorrow or in a few hours' or in a few moments' time. Jesus has a clear and direct approach:

That is why I am telling you not to worry about your life, and what you are to eat, nor about your body and what you are to wear. Surely life is more than food and the body more than clothing! Look at the birds in the sky. They do not sow or reap or gather into barns;

yet your heavenly Father feeds them. Are you not worth much more than they are? Can any of you, however much you worry, add one single cubit to your span of life? And why worry about clothing? Think of the flowers growing in the fields; they never have to work or spin; yet I assure you that not even Solomon in all his robes was clothed like one of these. Now if that is how God clothes the wild flowers growing in the field which are there today and thrown into the furnace tomorrow, will he not much more look after you, you who have so little faith. So do not worry; do not say 'What are we to eat? What are we to drink? What are we to wear?' It is the gentiles who set their hearts on all these things. Your heavenly father knows you need them all. Set your hearts on his kingdom first, and on God's saving justice, and all these other things will be given you as well. So do not worry about tomorrow: tomorrow will take care of itself. Each day has enough trouble of its own.

MATTHEW 6 J

Is it really possible to live in such a way? It would require the greatest trust in the love of God. There is no soft option. Luke clarifies the rigours of being a Christian disciple:

He called the twelve together and gave them power and authority over all devils and to cure diseases, and he sent them out to proclaim the kingdom of God and to heal. He said to them, 'Take nothing for the journey; neither staff, nor haversack, nor bread, nor money: and do not have a spare tunic. Whatever house you enter, stay there; and when you leave let your departure be from there. As for those who do not welcome you, when you leave their town shake the dust from your feet as evidence against them.' So they set out and went from village to village proclaiming the good news and healing everywhere.

LUKE 9 *J*

This is the passage which is said to have been St Francis' favourite text. He and a small band of followers sought to practise this and similar rules but, as his movement grew in number, many joined who were not prepared to follow his lead, and they undermined his authority until an easier discipline was established. St Francis may well have reflected ruefully on this next quotation:

The kingdom of heaven may be compared to a man who sowed good seed in his field. While everybody was asleep his enemy came, sowed darnel all among the wheat and made off. When the new wheat sprouted and ripened, then the darnel appeared as well. The owner's labourers went to him and said, 'Sir, was it not good seed that you sowed in your field? If so, where does the darnel come from?' He said to them, 'Some enemy has done this.' And the labourers said, 'Do you want us to go and weed it out?' But he said, 'No, because when you weed out the darnel you might pull up the wheat with it. Let it then grow till the harvest; and at harvest time I shall say to the reapers: First collect the darnel and tie it in bundles to be burnt, then gather the wheat into my barn.'

MATTHEW 13 *J*

There is nothing in this parable to suggest that the kingdom of heaven belongs to the future. What the future does seem to hold is the prospect of time coming to an end.

> The sower of the good seed is the Son of Man. The field is the world; the good seed is the subjects of the kingdom; the darnel, the subjects of the Evil One; the enemy who sowed it, the devil; the harvest is the end of the world; the reapers are the angels. Well then, just as the darnel is gathered up and burnt in the fire, so it will be at the end of time. The Son of Man will send his angels and they will gather out of his kingdom all causes of falling and all who do evil, and throw them into the blazing furnace.
>
> MATTHEW 13 J

This seems to support the idea of heaven present on earth. He says, 'The field is the world; the good seed is the subjects of the kingdom'; no doubt here – the subjects of the kingdom live in the world alongside everyone else. Only when the harvest is gathered, at 'the end of time', are the good and the evil sorted out from each other. In the following parables the same idea is given:

> Again the kingdom of Heaven is like a dragnet that is cast in the seas and brings in a haul of all kinds of fish. When it is full the fishermen haul it ashore; then sitting down they collect the good ones in baskets and throw away those that are no use. This is how it will be at the end of time: the angels will appear and

separate the wicked from the upright, to throw them into the blazing furnace, where there will be weeping and grinding of teeth.

MATTHEW 13 *J*

Then the kingdom of Heaven will be like this: Ten wedding attendants took their lamps and went to meet the bridegroom. Five of them were foolish and five were sensible: the foolish ones, though they took their lamps, took no oil with them, whereas the sensible ones took flasks of oil as well as their lamps. The bridegroom was late, and they all grew drowsy and fell asleep. But at midnight there was a cry, 'Look! the bridegroom! Go out and meet him.' Then all those wedding attendants woke up and trimmed their lamps, and the foolish ones said to the sensible ones, 'Give us some of your oil: our lamps are going out.' But they replied, 'There may not be enough for us and for you; you had better go to those who sell it and buy some for yourselves.' They had gone off to buy it when the bridegroom arrived. Those who were ready went in with him to the wedding hall and the door was closed. The other attendants arrived later. 'Lord, Lord,' they said, 'Open the door for us.' But he replied, 'In truth I tell you, I do not know you.' So stay awake, because you do not know either the day or the hour.

MATTHEW 25 *J*

The message of the last sentence could hardly be clearer for those of us who spend much of our time dreaming, or swallowing pills to help us sleep! There are moments in people's lives when quite literally time stands still. Most of us have experienced such a moment at some time and for many it is a moment of deep spiritual significance in which there is the greatest sense of wellbeing and release. For many it is as if the world becomes paper thin and people feel they can reach through and touch whatever lies beyond:

> Ask, and it will be given to you; search, and you will find; knock, and the door will be opened to you. Everyone who asks receives; everyone who searches finds; everyone who knocks will have the door opened. Is there anyone among you who would hand his son a stone when he asked for bread? Or hand him a snake when he asked for a fish?. If you, then, evil as you are, know how to give your children what is good, how much more will your Father in heaven give good things to those who ask him!
>
> MATTHEW 7 *J*

The message in this story from St Luke could not be clearer:

> Then he said to them, 'Watch, and be on your guard against avarice of any kind, for life does not consist in possessions, even when someone has more than he needs.' Then he told them a parable, 'There once was a rich man who, having had a good harvest from his land, thought to himself, "What am I to do? I have not enough room to store my crops." Then he said, "This is what I will do: I will pull down my barns and build bigger ones, and store all my grain and my goods in them, and I will say to my soul: My soul, you have plenty of good things laid by for many years to come;

take things easy, eat, drink, have a good time." But God said to him, "Fool! this very night the demand will be made for your soul; and this hoard of yours whose will it be then?" So it is when someone stores up treasure for himself instead of becoming rich in the sight of God.'

LUKE 12 *J*

CHAPTER 2

They that Mourn

*Blessed are they that mourn: for they
shall be comforted.*
AUTHORIZED VERSION

*Blessed are those who mourn:
they shall be comforted.*
NEW JERUSALEM BIBLE

*O the bliss of the man whose heart is broken for
the world's suffering and for his own sin,
for out of his sorrow he will find the joy of God!*
DAILY STUDY BIBLE

*You're blessed when you feel you've lost what is
most dear to you.
Only then can you be embraced by the
One most dear to you.*

THE MESSAGE

*God blesses those people who grieve.
They will find comfort!*

CONTEMPORARY ENGLISH VERSION

*Blessed are those in emotional turmoil;
they shall be united inside by love.*

PRAYERS OF THE COSMOS

*R*eading and reflecting on the biblical texts
brings the range of ideas and emotions close.
The sound of the voices seems so close; the experiences
are tangible. We have a sense that whatever we might
have to face in this life has been encountered by someone in a distant moment before us. In these moments
we can connect with what might be called a 'universal
time'. A time which belongs to everyone and which

connects everyone. To find it, all that is necessary is to let go of one's own personal time.

The congregation waits patiently. The coffin is borne quietly towards the altar. The minister intones the opening lines of the burial service: 'Blessed are they that mourn, for they shall be comforted ...' Most of us have heard these words on occasion. They form, perhaps, the best known Beatitude, yet it is difficult to make sense of it. Blessed *are* they that mourn – but how is one to be joyful and mournful at the same time?

The word 'mourn' is an old one. Its root is in Saxon and Anglo-Saxon words meaning 'to be anxious' or 'to pine away'. In the 16th century, 'mourning' began to be used to describe the clothes people wore when someone close had died. Gradually its association with bereavement developed so that today we think that to mourn is to lament the passing of someone close to us. In the Old Testament we find a broader meaning. This example is typical:

> The waters will ebb from the sea,
> the river will dry up and run low,
> the streams will become foul,
> the rivers of Egypt will stink and dry up.
> Rush and reed will turn black,
> the Nile-plants on the banks of the Nile
> will wither, blow away and will be no more.
> The fishermen will groan, it will be mourning
> for all who cast hook in Nile;
> those who spread nets on the waters will lose heart.
>
> ISAIAH 19 J

In the quotation above Isaiah prophesies a catastrophe in nature – the drying up of the river Nile on which the Egyptian economy depended. The Authorized Version translates this passage as:

> The fishers shall also mourn,
> and all they that cast angle into the brook shall
> lament, and they that spread nets upon the waters
> shall languish.

The mourning of fishermen would not be for the dead but for the pollution and eventual absence of the life-giving waters of the Nile.

Isaiah also predicts that Egypt will descend into civil war: 'they will fight with one another, brother against brother, friend against friend'.

The poet Jeremiah warns of God's retribution upon the Israelites. In response 'the earth will go into mourning':

> I looked to the earth – it was a formless waste;
> to the heavens, and their light had gone.
> I looked to the mountains – they were quaking
> and all the hills rocking to and fro.
> I looked – there was no one at all,
> the very birds of heaven had all fled,
> I looked – the fruitful land was a desert,
> all its towns in ruins
> before Yahweh,
> before his burning anger.
> Yes, Yahweh has said this,
> '

'The whole country will be laid waste,
though I shall not annihilate it completely.
For this, the earth will go into mourning
and the heavens above grow dark.'

JEREMIAH 4 *J*

And in the next quotation, the same poet speaks of a
city as if a woman, and describes her mourning:

How deserted she sits,
    the city once thronged with people!
Once the greatest of nations,
    she is now like a widow.
Once the princess of states,
    she is now put to forced labour.

The roads to Zion are in mourning;
    no one comes to her festivals now.
Her gateways are all deserted
    her priests groan
her young girls are grief stricken;
    she suffers bitterly.

LAMENTATIONS 1 *J*

Joel, a later prophet, who is said to have made the final
prophecies which included the visitation of the Holy
Spirit on Christ's apostles, writes of the effects of a
plague of locusts. He suggests that this is the army of
God bringing retribution to a recalcitrant Israel:

Listen to this, you elders;
everybody in the country attend!

Has anything like this ever happened in your day,
or in your ancestors' days?
Tell your children about it
and let your children tell their children,
and their children the next generation!

What the nibbler has left, the grown locust has eaten,
what the grown locust has left, the hopper has eaten,
and what the hopper has left, the shearer has eaten.

Wake up you drunkards, and weep!
All you wine-bibbers, lament
for the new wine: it has been snatched from
your lips.
For a nation has invaded my country,
mighty and innumerable,
with teeth like a lion's teeth,
with the fangs of a lioness.
It has reduced my vines to a desolation
and my fig trees to splinters,
stripped them and broken them down,
leaving their branches white.

Mourn, as a virgin-bride in sackcloth
for the bridegroom of her youth!
Cereal offering and libation
are lost to Yahweh's Temple.
The priests, the ministers of Yahweh,
are in mourning.
The fields are ruined,
the land is in mourning,
for the grain has been ruined,
the new wine has failed,
of olive oil only a trickle.

Stand dismayed, you farmers,
wail, you vinedressers,
for the wheat, for the barley!
The harvest of the fields has been lost!
The vine has withered,
the fig tree wilts away;
pomegranate, palm tree, apple tree,
every tree in the countryside is dry,
and for human beings
joy has run dry too.

JOEL 1 J

Jesus, a rabbinical teacher who many thought to be the Messiah, would have known this literature by heart. It was read and studied in every synagogue. This Beatitude would have awoken something deep in the heart of his Jewish listeners. There is a close association between a degraded land, bad husbandry and the word 'mourn'. It is clear that at times the Hebrew mind postulated the idea of a degraded mind being the close companion of a degraded land, as in this example:

Hear the word of the Lord, ye children of Israel, for the Lord hath a controversy with the inhabitants of the land, because there is no truth, nor mercy, nor knowledge of God in the land.

By swearing, and lying, and killing, and stealing and committing adultery, they break out, and blood toucheth blood.

Therefore shall the land mourn, and every one that dwelleth therein shall languish, with the beasts of the

fields and with the fowls of heaven; yea, the fishes of
the sea also shall be taken away.

HOSEA 4 *AV*

The Jews felt their religion and culture deeply. This
religion and the land on which they stood and had their
being were all connected through God. The land and
people were as family. The law, or at least behaviour
which flouted God's law, was also mourned. In this next
example, the emotion of hearing the law and recogniz-
ing the truth in it demonstrates just how close the law
and the people could be. The scribe Ezra reads to the
people 'from dawn until noon' the 'Book of the Law
of Moses'.

Then His Excellency Nehemiah and the priest-scribe
Ezra and the Levites who were instructing the people
said to all the people, 'Today is sacred to Yahweh your
God. Do not be mournful, do not weep.' For the
people were all in tears as they listened to the words
of the Law.

He then said, 'You may go; eat what is rich, drink
what is sweet and send a helping to the man who has
nothing prepared.' And the Levites calmed all the
people down, saying, 'Keep quiet: this is a sacred day.
Do not be sad.' Then all the people went off to eat and
drink and give helpings away and enjoy themselves to
the full, since they had understood the meaning of
what had been proclaimed to them.

NEHEMIAH 8 *J*

And here in Proverbs is the essence of it:

> When the righteous are in authority, the people
> rejoice: but when the wicked beareth rule, the people
> mourn.
>
> PROVERBS 29 AV

In this next example, considerations of the land and the
law are linked:

> How long will the land be in mourning, and the grass
> wither all over the countryside? The animals and birds
> are dying as a result of the wickedness of all the
> inhabitants.
>
> JEREMIAH 12 J

It is only when we begin to explore the usage of the
word 'comfort' that the significance of this next quotation becomes clear:

> The spirit of Lord Yahweh is on me
> for Yahweh has anointed me.
> He has sent me to bring the news to the afflicted,
> to soothe the broken hearted,
> to proclaim liberty to captives,
> release to those in prison,
> to proclaim a year of favour from Yahweh
> and a day of vengeance for our God,
> to comfort all who mourn,
> [to give to Zion's mourners]
> to give them for ashes, a garland;
> for mourning dress, the oil of gladness;
> for despondency, festal attire;

and they will be called terebinths* of 'saving justice',
planted by Yahweh to glorify him.

ISAIAH 61 J

* A terebinth is a beautiful tree from which turpentine is derived.

In using the phrase 'to comfort those who mourn,' Jesus
was quoting Isaiah whose words he loved and whose
prophesies he was to fulfil. The theme in Isaiah is
echoed in Job who makes it clear just who has the
power to heal sorrow. Here Job equates the power to lift
affliction with the power to give rain to dry earth. All
these things come from God.

Although affliction cometh not forth of the dust,
neither doth trouble spring out of the ground;

Yet man is born unto trouble, as the sparks fly
upward.

I would seek unto God, and unto God I would
commit my cause:

Which doeth great things and unsearchable;
marvellous things without number:

Who giveth rain upon the earth, and sendeth waters
upon the fields:

To set up on high those that be low; that those which
mourn may be exalted to safety.

JOB 5 AV

The *New Jerusalem Bible* translates the last sentence as:

> If his will is to raise up the downcast,
>   or exalt the afflicted to the heights of prosperity,
> he frustrates the plans of the artful
>   so that they cannot succeed in their intrigues.

> JOB 5 *J*

The best-known and most loved use of the word comes in Psalm 23, which is also associated with bereavement; it is read for comfort. It is quoted here in the familiar Authorized Version text:

> The Lord is my shepherd; I shall not want.

> He maketh me to lie down in green pastures: he leadeth me besides the still waters.

> He restoreth my soul: he leadeth me in the paths of righteousness for his name's sake.

> Yea, though I walk through the shadow of death, I will fear no evil: for thou art with me; thy rod and thy staff; they comfort me.

> Thou preparest a table before me in the presence of mine enemies: thou annointest my head with oil; my cup runneth over.

> Surely goodness and mercy shall follow me all the days of my life: and I will dwell in the house of the Lord for ever.

> PSALM 23 *AV*

A shepherd's rod or crook is there to keep discipline. It is used to grab the young lamb by neck or leg and yank it back to where it belongs. What we today call 'comfortable' is far from the sharp disciplinary action of the good shepherd. Once again the meaning of words is important. This view is confirmed in the following psalm in which the poet says that he has '... kept your age-old judgements in mind, Yahweh, and I am comforted'.

> Keep in mind your promise to your servant
> on which I have built my hope.
> It is my comfort in distress
> that your promise gives me life.
> Endlessly the arrogant have jeered at me,
> but I have not swerved from your Law
> I have kept your age-old judgements in mind,
> Yahweh, and I am comforted.
> Fury grips me when I see the wicked
> who abandon your Law.
> Your judgements are my song
> where I live in exile.
> All night, Yahweh, I hold your name in mind,
> I keep your Law.
> This is what it means to me,
> observing your precepts.

PSALM 119 J

So, here is a yearning for land and a yearning for law and the discipline to follow it, all of which are given by a merciful God:

Shout for joy, you heavens; earth exult!
Mountains, break into joyful cries!
For Yahweh has consoled his people,
is taking pity on his afflicted ones.

Look, I have engraved you on the palms of my
      hands,
your ramparts are ever before me
Your rebuilders are hurrying,
your destroyers and despoilers will soon go away.

ISAIAH 49 *J*

And again in this beautiful poem:

Rejoice with Jerusalem,
be glad for her, all you who love her!
Rejoice, rejoice with her,
all you who mourned her!

So that you may be suckled and satisfied
from her consoling breast,
so that you may drink deep with delight
from her generous nipple.

For Yahweh say this:
Look, I am going to send peace
flowing over her like a river,
and like a stream in spate
the glory of the nations.

You will be suckled, carried on her hip
and fondled in her lap.
As a mother comforts her child
so I shall comfort you;
you will be comforted in Jerusalem.

ISAIAH 66 *J*

This usage of the word comfort would have been most familiar to the disciples listening to Jesus. Later Jesus appears to have expanded its meaning. In St John, the Comforter is another word for the Holy Spirit. It carries the 'word' which is the knowledge of God spoken in time and beyond time. Its presence is dependent on the first sentence 'keep my commandments'. Comfort and discipline are as one:

> If ye love me, keep my commandments.

> And I will pray the Father, and he shall give you another Comforter, that he may abide with you for ever;

> Even the spirit of truth; whom the world cannot receive, because it seeth him not, neither knoweth him: but ye know him; for he dwelleth with you, and shall be in you.

> I will not leave you comfortless: I will come to you.

> Yet a little while, and the world seeth me no more; but ye see me: because I live, ye shall live also.

> At that day ye shall know that I am in my Father, and ye in me, and I in you.

JOHN 14 AV

CHAPTER 3
The Meek

Blessed are the meek: for they shall inherit the earth.

AUTHORIZED VERSION

Blessed are the gentle: they shall have the earth as inheritance.

NEW JERUSALEM BIBLE

O the bliss of the man who is always angry at the right time and never angry at the wrong time, who has every instinct, and impulse, and passion under control because he himself is God-controlled, who has the humility to realise his own ignorance and his own weakness, for such a man is a King among men!

DAILY STUDY BIBLE

*You're blessed when you're content with just who
you are – no more, no less.
That's the moment you find yourselves proud
owners of everything you can't buy.*

THE MESSAGE

*God blesses those people who are humble.
The earth will belong to them!*

CONTEMPORARY ENGLISH VERSION

*Healed are those who have wept inwardly with
the pain of repressed desire; they shall be renewed
in sympathy with nature.*

PRAYERS OF THE COSMOS

*T*he entry of Jesus into Jerusalem began a
sequence of events which would influence
world culture for the next 2,000 years. According to the
Gospellers, thousands lined the streets, strewing his
path with flowers and palms, and their cheers 'near
split the earth'. High expectations were in the air for
this man, who, spurning horse and chariot, the symbols
of cruel kings and emperors – as did his ancestor

Solomon – preferred to ride an ass and a colt, the humblest of beasts.

> Rejoice greatly, O daughter of Zion; shout, O
> daughter of Jerusalem: behold thy King cometh
> unto thee: He is just, and having salvation; lowly,
> and riding upon an ass, and upon a colt the foal of
> an ass.

> And I will cut off the chariot of Ephraim, and the
> horse from Jerusalem, and the battle bow shall be cut
> off: and he shall speak peace unto the heathen: and
> his dominion shall be from sea even to sea, and from
> the river even to the ends of the earth.

> As for thee also, by the blood of thy covenant I have
> sent forth thy prisoners out of the pit wherein there
> is no water.

> ZECHARIAH 9 *AV*

Was he the Messiah, the one who would deliver Israel from the tyrannical rule of Rome and bring 'truth, meekness and righteousness' to a vexed and suffering people?

> Gird thy sword upon thy thigh,
> O most mighty, with thy glory and thy majesty.
> And in thy majesty ride prosperously
>   because of truth and meekness and righteousness;
>   and thy right hand shall teach thee terrible things.

> PSALM 4 *J*

Was this the humble carpenter's son, 'Gentle Jesus, meek and mild', who had a natural gift for healing and a talent for homespun wisdom but was also a trouble-some crowd-puller and a threat to Roman civil peace and order?

> And in that day shall the deaf hear the words of the book, and the eyes of the blind shall see out of obscurity, and out of darkness.
>
> The meek also shall increase their joy in the Lord, and the poor among men shall rejoice in the Holy One of Israel.
>
> For the terrible one is brought to nought, and the scorner is consumed, and all that watch for iniquity are cut off …
>
> ISAIAH 29 *AV*

Could he really be the Son of God and the greatest of heroes – born in a manger, destined to defeat death, saviour of Jew and Gentile, and the willing servant of God's love, forgiveness and sacrifice – yet a man to bear all the sins of the world and lead his people to salvation at the 'end of days'?

> He had no form or charm to attract us,
> no beauty to win our hearts;
> he was despised, the lowest of men,
> a man of sorrows, familiar with suffering,
> one from whom as it were, we averted our gaze,
> despised, for whom we had no regard.
> Yet ours were the sufferings he was bearing,
> ours the sorrows he was carrying
> while we thought of him as someone being punished
> and struck with affliction by God;

> whereas he was being wounded for our rebellions,
> crushed because of our guilt ...

ISAIAH 53 J

Whatever kind of man he was, there is no doubt that the majority of Jews in Palestine were expecting the Messiah, the long-awaited One, foreseen by the prophets, who was to free Israel from evil and establish a new Jerusalem, a 'blessed' Jerusalem, in which God would take delight:

> For look, I am going to create new heavens and a
>   new earth,
>   and the past will not be remembered
>   and will come no more to mind.
> Rather be joyful, be glad for ever
>   at what I am creating,
>   for look, I am creating Jerusalem to be 'Joy'
>   and my people to be 'Gladness'.

* * * * *

> They will not toil in vain,
> nor bear children destined to disaster,
> for they are the race of Yahweh's blessed ones
> and so are their offspring.
> Thus, before they call I shall answer,
> before they stop speaking I shall have heard.
> The wolf and the young lamb will feed together,
> the lion will eat hay like the ox
> and dust be the serpent's food.
> No hurt, no harm will be done
> on all my holy mountain. Yahweh says.

ISAIAH 65 J

Throughout Jewish and Christian history runs a deep archetypal icon of meek virtue defeating the physically strong embodiment of evil. Whether Jesus was a militant victor, inspired artisan, or human manifestation of the divine, humble meekness is essential to his being for both Jews and, subsequently, Christians. The God in man, the Son of Man, the Son of God, was born in a manger and born to be king. St Paul was to write:

> Who, being in the form of God,
> did not count equality with God
> something to be grasped.
> Thus, he emptied himself,
> taking the form of a slave,
> becoming as human beings are;
> and in every way like a human being,
> he was humbler yet, even accepting death, death on
>   a cross.

PHILIPPIANS 2 *J*

And only a few years before in the Jewish community in Qumran, The Dead Sea Scrolls' record of the wise counsellors: 'They shall preserve the Faith in the land with steadfastness and meekness and shall atone for sin by the practice of justice and the suffering of sorrows of affliction …'

In Christianity and Judaism, much depends upon how the word 'meek' is understood. Unfortunately, its meaning is obscure. Jesus almost certainly used an Aramaic word which was translated into Greek and

Hebrew. The scholars of the Authorized Version chose to translate the Greek word as 'meek'. But in the 17th century, 'meek' had two meanings. The first conveyed 'gentle, courteous, kind and merciful'. The second meaning had a different quality, 'humble and submissive', which implies a certain weakness in the face of strength, and this is how we tend to use the word today.

The root of the Hebrew word means 'the afflicted', and one distinguished scholar defines the meek as 'the *fellahin* or poor of an oppressed country, living quiet lives under tyrannical and oppressive rulers'. His view suggests the word describes a social condition, rather than a 'spiritual' or emotional state of being. However, an Aramaic scholar suggests Jesus was using a word meaning 'one who has surrendered to God'. This view seems fully confirmed in the Old Testament texts. The people of Israel were to submit to God but not to other human beings, especially if they practised injustice which led to suffering. Jesus was speaking to the landless poor of Palestine whose lives and society were dominated by aggression and the cruellest of acts:

> Yahweh is about to try
> the elders and the princes of his people.
> 'You are the ones who have ravaged the vineyard,
> the spoils of the poor are in your houses.
> By what right do you crush my people
> And grind the faces of the poor?'
> says the Lord Yahweh Saboath.

ISAIAH 3 J

Thou didst cause judgement to be heard from
heaven; the earth feared and was still,

When God arose to judgement, to save all the meek
of the earth. Selah.

PSALM 76 *AV*

The tyrannized poor were certainly encouraged to
submit to the will of God, for in that lay the promise of
salvation. God would then visit his anger upon those
who were wicked. As Zephaniah, whose prophesy Jesus
fulfilled when entering Jerusalem, has it:

Seek ye the Lord, all ye meek of the earth, which
have wrought his judgement; seek righteousness,
seek meekness: it may be ye shall be hid in the day
of the Lord's anger.

ZEPHANIAH 2 *AV*

The emphasis upon virtuous poverty is reflected in this
psalm which combines condemnation of 'him who
prospereth', encouraging patience in those 'who wait
upon the Lord', with the promise which is repeated in
different forms throughout Hebrew scripture:

Rest in the Lord, and wait patiently for him:
fret not thyself because of him who prospereth in his
way, because of the man who bringeth wicked
devices to pass.

Cease from anger, and forsake wrath: fret not thyself
to do in any wise evil.

For evildoers shall be cut off: but those that wait
upon the Lord, they shall inherit the earth.

For yet a little while, and the wicked shall not be ...

But the meek shall inherit the earth; and shall delight
themselves in the abundance of peace.

PSALM 37 *AV*

So the 'oppressed poor' are waiting upon the Lord for
the 'New Jerusalem' which would not be long in
coming:

And they shall build the old wastes, they shall raise
up the former desolations, and they shall repair the
waste cities, the desolations of many generations.

ISAIAH 61 *AV*

All this is a far cry from the accustomed meaning of the
Beatitude. A vast array of literature, and human enlight-
enment and comfort, has been based upon a reading
which is both sentimental and romantic, and also a
clear distortion of what Jesus intended. But the word
'earth' is incorrect as well. The accurate translation is
'land'. Land, of course had great significance for the
Jews as it did for the English in the 17th century, many
of whom were being dispossessed by rapacious landlords. 'Blessed are the poor who wait upon the Lord, for
they shall inherit the Land'!

The word 'inherit' first appears in the Old Testament
in Genesis:

And he brought him forth abroad, and said, Look now toward heaven, and tell the stars, if thou be able to number them: and he said unto him, so shall thy seed be. And he believed in the Lord: and he counted it to him for righteousness. And he said unto him, I am the Lord that brought thee out of Ur of the Chaldees, to give thee this land to inherit it.

GENESIS 15 J

And later in Genesis, Jacob the tent dweller was sent to claim his inheritance:

And Isaac called Jacob, and blessed him and charged him, and said unto him, Thou shalt not take a wife of the daughters of Canaan.

Arise, go to Padan-aram, to the house of Bethuel thy mother's father; and take thee a wife from thence of the daughters of Laban thy mother's brother ...

And God Almightly bless thee, and make thee fruitful, and multiply thee, that thou mayest be a multitude of people;

And give thee the blessing of Abraham, to thee, and to thy seed with thee; that thou mayest inherit the land wherein thou art a stranger, which God gave unto Abraham.

GENESIS 28 AV

In Leviticus, God speaks to Moses confirming the intended land was to be inherited. Here it is in the graphic Authorized Version text:

Ye shall therefore keep all my statutes, and all my judgements, and do them: that the land, whither I bring you to dwell therein, spue you not out.

And ye shall not walk in the manners of the nation, which I cast out before you: for they committed all these things, and therefore I abhorred them.

But I have said unto you, Ye shall inherit their land, and I will give it unto you to possess it, a land that floweth with milk and honey: I am the Lord your God, which have separated you from other people.

LEVITICUS 20 *AV*

But once again things are not quite what they seem. In this next quotation we get some sense of what 'inheriting' land meant to the Israelites.

You will take possession of the country and settle in it, for I have given you the country as your property. You will share it out by lot among your clans. To a large clan you will give a larger heritage, and to a smaller clan you will give a smaller heritage. Where the lot falls for each, that will be his. Your heritage will depend on the size of your tribe.

NUMBERS 33 *J*

From the outset, the Israelites had been urged by Moses to share among themselves so that no one needed to suffer greater poverty than anyone else:

Is there anyone poor among you, one of your brothers, in any town of yours in the country which Yahweh your God is giving you? Do not harden your heart or close your hand against that poor brother of yours, but be open handed with him and lend him enough for his needs.

DEUTERONOMY 15 *J*

These are Yahweh's orders: Each of you must collect as much as he needs to eat – a homer per head for each person in his tent. The Israelites did this. They collected it, some more, some less. When they measured out what they had collected by the homer, no one who had collected more had too much, no one who had collected less had too little. Each had collected as much as he needed to eat.

EXODUS 16 *J*

This was 'care in the community', a sense of responsibility which belonged to everyone. Moses' conception of God's plan for the communal land was striking. The land was to be divided between the tribes and within the tribes according to the numerical strength of tribes and families. A process of casting lots decided which land would be allocated to tribe and family – God's will manifesting through the apparent chance of the lottery. The root of the word 'inherit' is 'lot'. To inherit was the process of allotting land by casting lots.

Inheriting land did not mean simply receiving it in a passive way. It meant to actively divide land by means of a lottery, safeguarded by ensuring each received sufficient according to his need. And once the land was allotted it was to be respected by all.

Thou shalt not remove thy neighbour's landmark,
which they of old time have set in thine inheritance,
which thou shalt inherit in the land that the Lord thy
God has giveth thee to possess it.

DEUTERONOMY 19 *AV*

thunders Deuteronomy.

Remove not the ancient landmark which thy fathers
have set.

PROVERBS 22 *AV*

Remove not the old landmark; and enter not into the
fields of the fatherless:

For their redeemer is mighty ...

PROVERBS 23 *AV*

threatens Proverbs.

In the Dead Sea Scrolls is a vitriolic reference to St
Paul, addressed as 'The Liar', in which he is accused of
'removing the boundary markers which the ancestors
have set down'. The leaders of Israel referred to this
system of tenure throughout Old Testament history:

Moses then gave the Israelites this order:

'This is the country where your heritages will be
assigned by lot, and which Yahweh has ordered to be
given to the nine tribes and the half-tribe.'

NUMBERS 34 *J*

Judges and officers shalt thou make thee in all thy gates, which the Lord thy God giveth thee, throughout thy tribes: and they shall judge the people with just judgment.

Thou shalt not wrest judgment; thou shalt not respect persons, neither take a gift: for a gift doth blind the eyes of the wise, and pervert the words of the righteous.

That which is altogether just shalt thou follow, that thou mayest live, and inherit the land which the Lord thy God giveth thee.

DEUTERONOMY 16 *AV*

And these are the countries which the children of Israel inherited in the land of Canaan, which Eleazar the priest, and Joshua the son of Nun, and the heads of the fathers of the tribes of the children of Israel, distributed for inheritance to them. By lot was their inheritance as the Lord commanded by the hand of Moses, for the nine tribes and for the half tribe.

DEUTERONOMY 14 *J*

The language used by the Authorized Version scholars has been interpreted in a way that Jesus' contemporaries would not have understood. We will look at possible reasons why they did this in the next chapter. These researches and reflections suggest that followers of Jesus would have understood this Beatitude to mean: 'Those poor and dispossessed of land who wait upon the Lord by obeying his laws, shall receive the land by lottery in the way of their forefathers and as commanded by God.'

These scriptural references enable us to gain a glimpse of early Jewish law defined by Moses and the later prophets. Jesus was rekindling the relationship between love of God and love of the land:

> Have you ever in your life given orders to the
> > morning
> > or sent the dawn to its post,
> to grasp the earth by its edges
> > and shake the wicked out of it.
> She turns it as red as a clay seal,
> > she tints it as though it were a dress,
> stealing the light from evil doers
> > and breaking the arm raised to strike.
> Have you been right down to the sources of the sea
> > and walked about at the bottom of the Abyss?
> Have you been shown the gates of Death,
> > have you seen the janitors of the Shadow dark
> > as death?
> Have you an inkling of the extent of the earth?
> > Tell me all about it if you have!
> Which is the way to the home of the Light,
> > and where does darkness live?
> You could then show them to their proper places,
> > you could put them on the path home again!
> If you do know, you must have been born when
> > they were,
> > you must be very old by now!

> JOB 38 J

The books of the Old Testament tell the history of the Jewish people's relationship with the earth, its land and water, verdant fields and deserts, seas and great rivers, and the glorious wealth which it all yields and the poverty which comes from its loss. It also tells the drama of the inconstant play of human ambition and sacrifice. Central to this great literature is the personal relationship which the Jews have with God, the provider of all things:

> The earth is the Lord's and the fullness thereof; the world and they that dwell therein.

> For he hath founded it upon the seas, and established it upon the floods.

> Who shall ascend into the hill of the Lord? or who shall stand in his holy place?

PSALM 24 *AV*

CHAPTER 4
Hunger and Thirst

Blessed are they which do hunger and thirst
after righteousness:
for they shall be filled.
AUTHORIZED VERSION

Blessed are those who hunger and thirst
for uprightness:
they shall have their fill.
NEW JERUSALEM BIBLE

O the bliss of the man who longs for total
righteousness as a starving man longs for food,
and a man perishing of thirst longs for water,
for that man will be truly satisfied.
DAILY STUDY BIBLE

You're blessed when you've worked up a good appetite for God. He's food and drink in the best meal you'll ever get.
THE MESSAGE BIBLE

God blesses those people who want to obey him more than to eat or drink.
CONTEMPORARY ENGLISH VERSION

Blessed are those who hunger and thirst for physical justice – righteousness;
they shall be surrounded by what is needed to sustain their bodies.
PRAYERS OF THE COSMOS

he Authorized Version of the Bible became available in English in 1611. Until that time it could only lawfully be read in Latin, a language available to a small ruling elite. In the early 14th century, Wyclif and others had made 'inspired attempts' at translating part of the texts. William Tyndale dedicated his life to translating, printing and distributing English language versions and was to be garrotted and burned at the stake for his efforts. Thousands of the Tyndale Bibles which had been smuggled into England from Holland and Belgium were ruthlessly hunted down and burned by the Bishop of London. Today only six copies survive.

Following the separation from Rome under Henry VIII a variety of religious sects had emerged, threatening the control of monarchy and aristocracy and the rule of law applied by local Justices of the Peace. Voltaire was to joke of the English that they were a nation of a hundred religions! Jesuit priests, seeking to revive Catholicism, were hunted down and often burned. Many extremist Protestants who threatened English political stability with Lutheran ideals also met dire fates.

It was a time when religion was central to political life. Usury, the practice of charging interest for credit or loans, was abolished by Act of Parliament in 1571. The debate at that time was dominated by argument about the meaning of God's word:

> He that putteth not out his money to usury, nor
> taketh reward against the innocent. He that doeth
> these things shall never be moved.
>
> PSALM 15 AV

In 1624 the Act was amended to permit usury. Hardly a 'word of God' was referred to during the second debate. The age of the secular economist was dawning.

Later in the 16th century, England faced a major economic crisis with high inflation and unemployment. Land enclosure transferred 'common and waste land' which had been used freely by the peasantry to private ownership. The peasants '... driven out of their habitations are forced into the great cities, where being burdensome, they shut their doors against them, suffering them to die in the streets and highways' (Sir Anthony Cope to Lord Burleigh). Crime increased and the common people fell into misery and poverty.

Since most of the enclosed land was put to pasture the main 'improvement' was the increase in rent which was obtained by the new landlords. The character of this period of English history has been described as 'the worship of Mammon: company promoters, clerical cupidity, speculators, embezzlers, land hunger, litigiousness and lawlessness' (Prof J P Black, *Oxford History of England*).

It was within this social context that King James approved an English language translation of the Bible to suit the political taste of the English ruling classes. As the translators of the King James Version said:

> Happy is the man that delighteth in the scripture, and thrice happy that meditateth in it night and day. But how shall men meditate in that which they cannot understand?

In the social conditions which prevailed at the time, how were the Beatitudes to be treated? What would the third Beatitude suggest if it were translated as 'Blessed are the poor who wait upon the Lord: for they shall inherit the land'? How would it be understood by the significant number of English peasants who were being thrown off the land by powerful and very often corrupt landlords? These were difficult times: Tyndale, Sir Thomas More, Cranmer and Latimer were all burned or beheaded in the name of religion. What were the starving peasantry of England to make of the following text?

> Is there anyone poor among you, one of your brothers, in any town of yours in the country which Yahweh your God is giving you? Do not harden your heart or close your hand against that poor brother of yours, but be open handed with him and lend him enough for his needs. Do not allow this mean thought in your heart and give him nothing; he could appeal against you to Yahweh, and you would incur guilt. When you give to him, you must give with an open heart; for this, Yahweh your God will bless you in all your actions and all your undertakings. Of course there will never cease to be poor people in the country, and this is why I am giving you this command: always be open handed with your brother, and with anyone in your country who is in need and poor.
>
> DEUTERONOMY 15 J

Of course, such passages may have helped establish the first 'Poor Laws' for 'the deserving poor'. Yet it is clear who the land belonged to and it wasn't the landlords! The land belonged to God:

> The land shall not be sold for ever: for the land is
> mine; for ye are strangers and sojourners with me.
>
> LEVITICUS 25 *AV*

The text goes on to state that even when the ancestral
land has been sold because of poverty, it could be
redeemed by the family in return for compensation:

> At the end of every seven years, you must grant remis-
> sion. The nature of the remission is as follows: any
> creditor holding a personal pledge obtained from his
> fellow must release him from it: he must not exploit
> his fellow or brother once the latter has appealed to
> Yahweh for remission. A foreigner you may exploit,
> but you must remit whatever claim you have on your
> brother. There must, then, be no poor among you. For
> Yahweh will grant you his blessing in the country
> which Yahweh your God is giving you to possess as
> your heritage, only if you pay careful attention to the
> voice of Yahweh your God, by keeping and practising
> all these commandments which I am enjoining on
> you today.
>
> DEUTERONOMY 15 *J*

The Israelites regularly failed to do this. Some centuries
later, Ezekiel was proposing the same system of tenure:

> The Lord Yahweh says this, 'This will be the territory
> which you must distribute among the twelve tribes of
> Israel, with two portions for Joseph. You will each
> have a fair share of it, since I swore to your fathers that
> I would give it to them, and this country now falls to
> you as your heritage. These will be the frontiers of the

country. On the north, from the Great Sea ... the road from the Pass of Hamath; that will be the western frontier. You must distribute this country among yourselves, among the tribes of Israel. You must distribute it as a heritage for yourselves and the aliens settled among you who have fathered children among you, since you must treat them as citizens of Israel. They must draw lots for their heritage with you, among the tribes of Israel. You will give the alien his heritage in the tribe where he has settled' – declares the Lord Yahweh.

EZEKIEL 47 J

These texts influenced religious and political movements in the 17th century. The Diggers, led by Gerrard Winstanley, observed that power in England came from ownership of land. They maintained that the land belonged to everyone, rich and poor, and that those who wished to work had an inalienable right of access to land. In one of their pamphlets, titled 'A New Law of Righteousness', it was held that private property in land had brought about dire poverty.

A Digger group from a village in Northamptonshire declared in a petition: 'We find that no creature that ever God made was ever deprived of the benefit of the Earth but Mankind ...' After describing the terrible plight their small town had fallen into, they announced: '... we consider that the Earth is our Mother; and that God hath given it to the children of men; and that the Common and Waste Grounds belong to the poor;

and that we have a right to the common ground both from the law of the land, Reason, and scriptures.' They went on to state that they would not dig land that belonged to others without permission. The petition was reported to the Council of State in London which immediately ordered that the villagers be arrested and sent for trial.

Perhaps it was understandable that the committee of bishops and scholars who were chosen to translate the Greek and Hebrew texts into common English regarded the word 'justice' with some diffidence. The nature of justice lies at the heart of English social and legal conscience. The Greek word used by Matthew in this Beatitude means justice. But the translators discovered 'righteous', a little-used word at the time which carried a spiritual quality and would divert attention from the politically dangerous territory which 'justice' might evoke.

Justice is used in the Authorized Version some 24 times; righteousness is used over 450 times. Later revised editions of the Bible often exchanged the word 'uprightness' for 'righteousness', as does a modern translation like the *New Jerusalem Bible*. Often the Jerusalem uses the expression 'saving justice', where the Authorized Version uses righteousness. In Hebrew the word for justice and righteousness is the same, but the subtlety of Hebrew does permit a translation of 'a righteous man' as one 'who follows the law with humility, mitigating justice with mercy'.

Here are two examples of the verse in Isaiah 51 on which this Beatitude is said by scholars to be based:

Hearken to me, ye that follow after righteousness,
ye that seek the Lord.

AV

Listen to me, you who pursue saving Justice,
you who seek Yahweh.

J

The context in which justice, righteousness or upright-ness are used provides some wonderful biblical language and poetry:

On hearing me, people congratulated me,
    on seeing me, people deferred to me,
because I freed the poor in distress
    and the orphan who had no helper.
The dying man's blessing rested on me
    and I gave the widow's heart cause to rejoice.
Uprightness I wore as a garment,
    fair judgement was my cloak and my turban.
I was eyes for the blind,
    and feet for the lame.
Who but me was father of the poor?
    The stranger's case had a hearing from me.
I used to break the fangs of the wicked,
    and snatch their prey from their jaws.

JOB 29 *J*

In this next psalm the poet reminds us of how man falls short of the perfection which God's justice demands:

Yahweh, who can find a home in your tent,
who can dwell on your holy mountain?

Whoever lives blamelessly,
who acts uprightly,
who speaks the truth from the heart,
who keeps the tongue under control,

who does not wrong a comrade,
who casts no discredit on a neighbour,
who looks with scorn on the vile,
but honours those who fear Yahweh,

who stands by an oath at any cost,
who asks no interest on loans,*
who takes no bribe to harm the innocent.
No one who so acts can ever be shaken.

PSALM 15 J

* *See* Chapter 5.

In this passage from Proverbs, Wisdom speaks of her love for justice, suggesting that the riches justice brings are worth more than gold and silver:

I, Wisdom, share house with Discretion,
    I am mistress of the art of thought.
[Fear of Yahweh means hatred of evil.]
I hate pride and arrogance,
    wicked behaviour and a lying mouth.
To me belong good advice and prudence,
    I am perception; power is mine!
By me monarchs rule
    and princes decree what is right;

by me rulers govern,
    so do nobles, the lawful authorities.
I love those who love me;
    whoever searches eagerly for me finds me.
With me are riches and honour,
    lasting wealth and saving justice.
The fruit I give is better than gold, even the finest,
    the return I make is better than pure silver.

I walk in the way of uprightness
    in the path of justice,
to endow my friends with my wealth
    and to fill their treasuries.

PROVERBS 8 *J*

There can be no doubt that justice was to be the foundation of the 'New Jerusalem', anticipated by all Jews and to be established by the Messiah:

Open for me the gates of saving justice,
I shall go in and thank Yahweh.
This is the gate of Yahweh,
where the upright go in.
I thank you for hearing me,
and making yourself my Saviour.

The stone which the builders rejected
has become the cornerstone;
This is Yahweh's doing,
and we marvel at it.
This is the day which Yahweh has made,
a day for us to rejoice and be glad.

PSALM 118 *J*

Except for this Beatitude, the Gospellers fail to record Jesus making a direct reference to justice (although it is a constant theme of St Paul). Of course many of the sayings of Jesus and the parables imply justice and demonstrate how he understood it.

The concept of a promised land for Israel extends back to Abraham. God promised land in exchange for the Israelites keeping God's law which was announced to Moses. It is inconceivable that Jesus would not have addressed this issue. In Luke we find one of the few references to this subject:

> He … went into the synagogue on the Sabbath day as he usually did. He stood up to read, and they handed him the scroll of the prophet Isaiah. Unrolling the scroll he found the place where it is written:
>
>> The spirit of the Lord is on me,
>> for he has anointed me
>> to bring the good news to the afflicted.
>> He has sent me to proclaim liberty to captives,
>> sight to the blind,
>> to let the oppressed go free,
>> to proclaim a year of favour from the Lord.
>
> Then he rolled up the scroll, gave it back to the assistant and sat down. And all eyes in the synagogue were fixed on him. Then he began to speak to them, 'This text is being fulfilled today even while you are listening.' And he won the approval of all, and they were astonished by the gracious words which came from his lips.

St Luke 4 *J*

Jesus goes on to say that 'Heaven remained shut' for three years during Elisha's time – a period when the Israelites were failing to follow the law of God. The congregation became so angry that they tried to throw Jesus off a nearby cliff. What was special about this incident and why did Luke want to record it? Jesus had carefully selected a quotation from Isaiah, but he stopped reading it in mid-sentence:

> The spirit of Lord Yahweh is on me
> For Yahweh has anointed me.
> He has sent me to bring the news to the afflicted,
> to soothe the broken hearted,
> to proclaim liberty to captives,
> release to those in prison,
> to proclaim a year of favour from Yahweh ...

At this point Jesus stopped. Nothing could be more calculated to emphasize the verse *'to proclaim a year of favour from Yahweh'*. The unread part of the quotation continues:

> and a day of vengeance for our God,
> to comfort all who mourn,
> to give them for ashes, a garland;
> for mourning-dress, the oil of gladness;
> for despondency, festal attire;
> and they will be called terebinths of 'saving justice',
> planted by Yahweh to glorify him.

ISAIAH 61 J

The passage in Luke 4 receives much attention for it declares the ministry of Jesus. Translated from the

Hebrew the expression 'to proclaim a year of favour' means 'a year of Grace'. There can be little doubt that Jesus, as Isaiah before him, was referring to the jubilee year, when land is brought to rest in fallow and returned to those who originally 'inherited' it. This was also a time when all debts were forgiven:

> This fiftieth year will be a year of jubilee for you; in it you will not sow or harvest the grain … or gather grapes from your untrimmed vine. The jubilee will be a holy thing for you. In the jubilee each of you will return to his ancestral property … you will not exploit one another, but fear your God, for I am Yahweh your God … Hence you will put my laws into practice, and you will live securely in the country.
>
> LEVITICUS 25 J

The idea that Jesus, the very Son of God, was recommending that land should be 'de-privatized' and returned to the people every fifty years was explosive at a time when the land of England was being enclosed for private benefit. We have seen that the prophets were well aware of the importance of this aspect of justice. It was a condition of God's gift of land to the Israelites. The poor, the meek and the mournful would certainly, and quite literally, hunger and thirst for the re-establishment of the grace of this jubilee.

Land ownership and power go together, as much now as in Jesus' day. Those with power are never likely to yield up control of land. There can be little doubt that Jesus was reminding his society that justice required the people to remember that the land belonged to God and could not be sold forever, and that it had to be returned to the people at regular intervals. This was not the only aspect of justice which concerned Jesus. Mercy and forgiveness were also vital contributions to a God-fearing society.

CHAPTER 5
The Merciful

Blessed are the merciful: for they shall obtain mercy.
AUTHORIZED VERSION

*Blessed are the merciful: they shall have mercy
shown them.*
NEW JERUSALEM BIBLE

*O the Bliss of the man who gets right
inside other people,
until he can see with their eyes, think with their
thoughts, feel with their feelings.
For he who does that will find others do
the same for him,
and will know that is what God in
Jesus Christ has done!*
DAILY STUDY BIBLE

*You're blessed when you care. At the moment
of being 'care-full'
you find yourselves being cared for.*
THE MESSAGE BIBLE

*God blesses those people who are merciful.
They will be treated with mercy!*
CONTEMPORARY ENGLISH VERSION

*Healthy are those who extend a long heartfelt
breath where ever needed;
they shall find their own prayer answered.*
PRAYERS OF THE COSMOS

*T*he exercise of spiritual reflection, described in the Introduction, focuses on economic issues and this raises an important question: Why does the world of economics seem an unsuitable subject for spiritual reflection? Most of us think that meditation, reflection and prayer are 'spiritual' activities. Things like work, and feeding, housing and clothing ourselves, are to do with our 'earthly existence' or our 'worldly objectives', which are secular and quite distinct from our spiritual concerns. One belongs to the outer world, the other to the inner.

The American environmentalist and philosopher, Wendell Berry, describes in his essay 'The Body and the Earth' how we have separated 'body' from 'soul' so that the qualities of the soul and the light of the spirit reflected in the soul to nourish us are diffused. The body, the earth and the whole material realm obscure its divinity. The consequences of this separation include violence to the earth and its creatures, violence to nature in the agricultural and environmental sense, and isolation and loneliness for so many human beings. This artificial division, this mental schism between body and soul, has long been established in Christianity, but its cause is not to be found in the teachings of Jesus. It has more to do with human psychology than religion, although as Christianity developed, fusing together all manner of cultural ideas and practices, it created conditions for this separation to grow and spread throughout Christendom and beyond.

Of course, we are encouraged to see God in our work and our recreation, in the daily context of marriage, parentage and friendship. We strain our eyes for the divine presence, which all too often seems very well concealed, and so we tire of the effort and forget. Is this not because we want to manage God as we manage everything else in our lives? We reduce God in size. We try to find God *in* our work instead of considering our work, when we are working, as the *presence* of God. We prefer to think that God is *in* everything. In practice we cannot conceive that He *is* everything.

This minimizing of God is so habitual that to many minds it is blasphemous to worship sunlight, air, water and land, or the incalculable combinations of these elements which present themselves to us in every waking moment. These things are part of 'my' world, my experience, my possessions, my universe. 'I'll do it my way!' Therefore, God is separate and has no part of this; He is out there, up there, over there, in there and beyond there! Anywhere but here. A separate God, divided from us; a God we have to find. And when we tire of looking, a God who does not exist.

Yet, in the Beatitudes, and in the Sermon on the Mount as a whole, Jesus, with the authority of Moses and the prophets, reminds us that our division of the world into mutually exclusive bodies and souls is false. In the Beatitudes Jesus was reminding Jews how to live a heavenly life on earth. This was not a 'lifestyle' which he invented but one which had been given to Moses and restated by the prophets.

In his book *The Passover Plot*, Hugh Schonfield writes:

> We are compelled by the evidence at our command ...
> to think of him as a man with very definite spiritual
> convictions who treated the Bible as the incontro-
> vertible Word of God.

That 'incontrovertible Word' was to be sounded, heard and obeyed on land; the dry surface of the planet without which there can be no living for Jews or for anyone else. And the fundamental law given for all to remember is to recognize that the land, and all that comes from it, belongs to God:

> The earth is the Lord's and the fullness thereof.
>
> PSALM 24 *AV*

It is an unequivocal statement. It does not admit of any prior claim. It has the full recognition of Jesus and is expressed poetically in the mysterious Gospel of St Thomas:

> Lift a stone and I am there, cleave a piece of wood and I am there.

God is universally present and not a 'thing' to be discovered by rummaging around life's filing cabinet. He is a living presence constantly available to us. The way we deny this simplicity is to insert the idea of possession, as for example in, 'It is *my* body and I'll do what I like with it!' The simple word 'my' claims the whole material world, the emotional world and any other world we care to add to our collection.

The first economists saw things in a different way: According to Quesnay, the 17th-century French philosopher and father of economics:

> God has endowed the universe with a physical constitution by which everything is ordered in nature …

> It is God who gives us the power to study and to discover the link between cause and effect that establishes natural laws ... [which are] the essential conditions according to which everything operates in the order prescribed by the author of nature.

Quesnay had an explicit maxim for this. It states:

> From nature: right order, and laws; from men: caprice, regulation and coercion.

Yet caprice, regulation and coercion have come to dominate the world of economics, business, science and politics. Wealth creation and distribution have created a Godless kingdom. Little wonder that the idea of reflecting, meditating, contemplating or even praying about such things seems absurd – a denial even. Whereas the primal human, described by Laurens van der Post as 'the first human', sees God in trees, rocks and springs of water, we have created a world of work without any reference to the 'author of nature'. And it has become a voracious dragon, seemingly out of control. The first simple division of body from soul has become cancerous, and the rapid growth of this division is poisoning the essentials of life: the air we breathe, the water we drink, the food we eat, and the land from which our bodies are drawn.

This current state of our world is not dissimilar to the state of the Roman world at the time of Jesus. He was contending with a cruel tyrannical rule from Rome and a corrupt and hypocritical religious priesthood which was leading the Jewish people deeper into an age of materialism. If he was the Messiah or the Son of God, he would have known what consequences would follow. He certainly knew that Moses and the prophets reported that God would wreak vengeance on a people who willfully disobeyed His law. The prophets conceived that the history of the Jews demonstrates to all that if God's law is ignored, retribution follows.

And yet there was something else within the tradition which Jesus proclaimed. In itself it was miraculous and defied reason. It was reasonable for the Jews to hold that justice required vengeance upon those who offended the law. Yet they had discovered that true supplication to God evoked mercy:

> Do not be stubborn like your ancestors. Submit to Yahweh, come to his sanctuary which he has consecreted for ever, and serve Yahweh your God, so that his fierce anger may turn away from you. For if you return to Yahweh, your brothers and your sons will be treated mercifully by their captors and be allowed to return to this country; for Yahweh your God is gracious and merciful and will not turn his face away from you, if you return to him.
>
> 2 CHRONICLES 30 J

In this mysterious process of sincerely turning to God, the consequences of our actions might be changed:

> We have not listened to your servants the prophets, who spoke in your name to our kings, our chief men, our ancestors and all people of the country.

Saving justice, Lord, is yours; we have only the look of shame we wear today, we, the people of Judah, the inhabitants of Jerusalem, the whole of Israel, near and far away, in every country to which you have dispersed us because of the treachery we have committed against you. To us, our kings, our chief men and our ancestors, belongs the look of shame, O Yahweh, since we have sinned against you. And it is for the Lord our God to have mercy and to pardon, since we have betrayed him, and have not listened to the voice of Yahweh our God nor followed the laws he has given us through his servants the prophets. The whole of Israel has flouted your Law and turned away, unwilling to listen to your voice; and the curse and imprecation written in the Law of Moses, the servant of God, have come pouring down on us because we have sinned against him.

DANIEL 9 *J*

In the Authorized Version, the second half of this passage is translated differently. It suggests the calamity which has beset 'the men of Judah' and the inhabitants of Jerusalem is justified, 'because of their trespass that they have trespassed against thee' – familiar words. It continues by establishing that it is God who is the source of mercy and forgiveness to those who trespass: 'to us [the Israelites] belongeth confusion of face … because we have sinned against thee. To the Lord our God belong mercies and forgivenesses …'

It comes as a surprise that the words 'forgiveness' and 'trespass' are rarely used in the Gospels. 'Trespass' occurs in just four contexts, all of which are concerned with forgiveness. The most familiar usage is in the Lord's Prayer. There are two principal versions of this prayer, although there are significant variations between the Authorized Version and more recent translations.

In St Luke we read:

Our Father which art in heaven, Hallowed be thy name. Thy kingdom come. Thy will be done, as in heaven, so in earth.

Give us day by day our daily bread.

And forgive us our sins; for we also forgive every one that is indebted to us. And lead us not into temptation; but deliver us from evil.

LUKE 11 *AV*

Luke then develops the narrative to the passage 'Ask and it shall be given'.

In St Matthew the prayer is included in the Sermon on the Mount in a section where guidance is given regarding prayer:

Our Father which art in heaven, Hallowed be thy name.

Thy kingdom come. Thy will be done in earth, as it is in heaven.

Give us this day our daily bread.

And forgive us our debts, as we forgive our debtors.

And lead us not into temptation, but deliver us from evil: For thine is the kingdom, and the power, and the glory, for ever. Amen.

MATTHEW 6 *AV*

The prayer is immediately followed by:

> For if ye forgive men their trespasses, your heavenly
> Father will also forgive you ...

The sense of this is the same as:

> Blessed are the merciful: for they shall receive mercy.

Although many of us use 'trespasses' in the Lord's
Prayer, it appears only in Tyndale's translation of 1534:

> Give us this day our daily bread.
> And forgive us our trespasses,
> even as we forgive our trespassers ...

But the Greek word for trespass does not appear at all
in the prayer. The Greek word in the prayer means
'debt' and its primary meaning is 'financial debt'. Why
would Jesus ask his followers to forgive debts?

The conditions concerning lending of money had
been closely drawn by Moses. The charging of interest
was forbidden:

> If you lend money to any of my people, to anyone
> poor among you, you will not play the usurer with
> him: you will not demand interest from him.
>
> EXODUS 22 J

This was a time when unpaid debts would lead directly
to being sold into slavery. The law of Moses forbade this
happening:

> If your brother becomes impoverished and cannot
> support himself in the community, you will assist him
> as you would a stranger or guest, so that he can go on

living with you. Do not charge him interest on a loan
... You will not lend him money on a loan or give him
food to make a profit out of it ... If your brother
becomes impoverished while with you and sells himself to you, you will not make him do the work of a
slave; you will treat him like an employee or guest, and
he will work for you until the jubilee year. He will then
leave you, both he and his children, and return to his
clan and regain possession of his ancestral property.

LEVITICUS 25 J

Secondly, all loans, all debts were to be forgiven every
seventh year, irrespective of whether they had been
repaid or not:

At the end of every seven years you must grant remission. The nature of the remission is as follows: any
creditor holding a personal pledge obtained from his
fellow must release him from it; he must not exploit
his fellow or his brother once the latter has appealed
to Yahweh for remission. A foreigner you may exploit,
but you must remit whatever claim you have on your
brother. There must, then, be no poor among you.

DEUTERONOMY 15 J

This was a radical way of ensuring that the Israelite
community were free of the mountainous debts which
we, today, take for granted. It is hardly an approval of
a credit card economy. 'Forgive us our debts as we
forgive our debtors' was a sharp reminder to his
disciples of the law which required the exercise of great
mercy as well as sacrifice.

All this is confirmed by Jesus in St Luke's abbreviated version of the Sermon on the Mount:

> But I say this to you who are listening: love your enemies, do good to those who hate you, bless those who curse you, pray for those who treat you badly ... Give to everyone who asks you and do not ask for your property back from someone who takes it. Treat others as you would like people to treat you ... And if you do good to those who do good to you, what credit can you expect? For even sinners do that much. And if you lend to those from whom you hope to get money back, what credit can you expect? Even sinners lend to sinners to get back the same amount. Instead, love your enemies and do good to them, and lend without any hope of return.
>
> LUKE 6 J

In both St Luke and St Matthew the idea and practice of mercy is taken further in the Sermon:

> For if ye forgive men their trespasses, your heavenly Father will also forgive you:
>
> But if ye forgive not men their trespasses, neither will your Father forgive your trespasses.
>
> MATTHEW 6 AV

The Greek word for 'trespass' certainly does not mean debt. It can best be translated as 'straying from the way' or 'missing the mark'. The Dead Sea Scrolls accuse St Paul of 'leading astray in a trackless desert'. It could be that Tyndale used this word in its old French meaning of 'missing the mark' or 'missing the way'. What is clear is that debt and missing the mark are quite distinct. The meaning of 'forgive' is also obscure. One scholar has suggested that the concept of forgiveness was unknown before Jesus. Until then actions were either condemned or condoned.

What is beyond doubt in Jesus' teaching is that the forgiving will receive forgiveness, the merciful shall receive mercy. Those who do not judge will avoid judgement and those who 'raise themselves up' will be humbled while those who are humble will be 'raised up'. The Gospels are full of examples of what is called reciprocity. It is like a seesaw, pivoted upon something which flows from God to his people. There can be little doubt that any society in which these injunctions are practised would be full of love and gratitude. In fact the word 'mercy' is related to the Latin word for 'thanks'.

A dictionary definition says that mercy is 'compassion shown by one person to another who is in his power and who has no claim to receive kindness', but Jesus suggests mercy invariably flows from God when people turn fully to Him with complete sincerity in their hearts. It is not difficult to find people who have experienced this flow at specific moments. What is difficult to find is anyone who would admit to living a merciful life.

One sure sign that mercy is diminished in our communities is the way we are prepared to sue in courts of law, doctors, nurses, or anyone else responsible for the care of others. Excess litigation is a sure sign of a disintegrating society.

This Beatitude reminds us that all activities in society are part of a unity and that we are all part of the same unity. It goes further than the Mosaic law which waits every seventh or forty-ninth year to redress injustices. Jesus asks for a constant practice. To those who do practise the loving discipline of forgiveness and mercifulness, God's mercy is ever available. Those who separate themselves from the unity, receive justice without mercy. Jesus spoke the following parable to certain people who prided themselves on being upright and despised everyone else:

> Two men went up to the Temple to pray, one a Pharisee, the other a tax collector. The Pharisee stood there and said this prayer to himself, 'I thank you, God, that I am not grasping, unjust, adulterous like everyone else, and particularly that I am not like this tax collector here. I fast twice a week; I pay tithes on all I get.' The tax collector stood some distance away, not daring even to raise his eyes to heaven; but he beat his breast and said, 'God, be merciful to me, a sinner.' This man, I tell you, went home again justified; the other did not. For everyone who raises himself up will be humbled, but anyone who humbles himself will be raised up.
>
> LUKE 18 J

Jesus is encouraging a common practice in the regulation of our daily lives. Perhaps it is time that Justice, Forgiveness and Mercy were found in the indexes of our economics and management studies text books. In the Catholic Church, Mary is seen symbolically as the

Earth and the Material Creation. Mary recognizes God in all things and gives him praise:

And Mary said, My soul doth magnify the Lord.

And my spirit hath rejoiced in God my Saviour.

For he hath regarded the low estate of his handmaiden: for, behold, from henceforth all generations shall call me blessed.

For he that is mighty hath done to me great things; and holy is his name.

And his mercy is on them that fear him from generation to generation.

He hath shewed strength with his arm; he hath scattered the proud in the imagination of their hearts.

He hath put down the mighty from their seats, and exalted them of low degree.

He hath filled the hungry with good things; and the rich he hath sent empty away.

He hath holpen his servant Israel, in remembrance of his mercy;

As he spake to our fathers, to Abraham, and to his seed for ever.

LUKE 1 *AV*

CHAPTER 6
The Pure in Heart

*Blessed are the pure in heart: for they
shall see God.*
AUTHORIZED VERSION

*Blessed are the pure in heart: for they
shall see God.*
NEW JERUSALEM BIBLE

*O the bliss of the man whose motives are
absolutely pure,
for that man will some day be able to see God.*
DAILY STUDY BIBLE

*You're blessed when you get inside your world –
your heart and mind – put right.
Then you can see God in the outside world.*

THE MESSAGE BIBLE

*God blesses those people whose hearts are pure.
They will see him!*

CONTEMPORARY ENGLISH VERSION

*Blessed are the consistent in heart; they shall
contemplate the One.*

PRAYERS OF THE COSMOS

*T*here are just two references in the Gospels
and the Old Testament to a 'pure heart';
one is in this Beatitude, the other in the magnificent
Psalm 24, which although relatively short has a wide
compass.

> The earth is the Lord's and the fulness thereof; the
> world, and they that dwell therein.

> For he hath founded it upon the seas, and
> established it upon the floods.

Who shall ascend into the hill of the Lord? or who shall stand in his holy place?

He that hath clean hands, and a pure heart; who hath not lifted up his soul unto vanity, nor sworn deceitfully.

He shall receive the blessing from the Lord, and righteousness from the God of his salvation.

This is the generation of them that seek him, that seek thy face, O Jacob.* Selah.

Lift up your heads, O ye gates; and be ye lift up, ye everlasting doors; and the King of glory shall come in.

Who is this King of glory? The Lord strong and mighty, the Lord mighty in battle.

Lift up your heads, O ye gates; even lift them up, ye everlasting doors; and the King of glory shall come in.

Who is this King of glory? The Lord of hosts, he is the King of glory. Selah.

PSALM 24 *AV*

* The literal meaning here is 'the face of Jacob's God'.

The psalm is also in harmony with the opening of the Gospel of St John:

In the beginning was the Word, and the Word was with God, and the Word was God.

The same was in the beginning with God.

All things were made by him; and without him was not anything made that was made.

In him was life; and the life was the light of men.

And the light shineth in darkness; and the darkness comprehended it not.

ST JOHN 1 *AV*

The question in Psalm 24, 'Who shall ascend the hill of the Lord?' is in effect asking who is qualified to comprehend the light? The answer is certain: those with clean hands and pure hearts, those not devoted to pleasure and triviality and who do not deceive themselves or others. The 'light' or glory of God is awesome, and various warnings are given throughout Hebrew scripture not to look directly upon the face of God:

He then said, 'Please show me your glory.' Yahweh said, 'I shall make all my goodness pass before you, and before you I shall pronounce the name Yahweh; and I am gracious to those to whom I am gracious and I take pity on those on whom I take pity.' 'But my face,' he said, 'you cannot see, for no human being can see me and survive.' Then Yahweh said, 'Here is a place near me. You will stand on the rock, and when my glory passes by, I shall put you in a cleft of the rock and shield you with my hand until I have gone past. Then I shall take my hand away and you will see my back; but my face will not be seen.'

EXODUS 33 *J*

But Psalm 24 says that those with a pure heart receive a blessing from the Lord. Such people are a generation who seek the face of the God of Jacob. 'To seek the face of God' is a Hebrew expression which means to seek to know God and live in His presence. We find it used again in this next psalm as the poet sings of the desire of the heart for union with God:

> Yahweh, hear my voice as I cry,
>   pity me, answer me!
> Of you my heart has said,
>   'Seek his face!'
> Your face, Yahweh, I seek;
>   do not turn away from me.

PSALM 27 J

Scholars say that 'seeking the face', seeking the presence of God, is the Old Testament equivalent of the expression Jesus used in his preaching: 'seek ye the kingdom of heaven'. To those listening to Jesus the two expressions would be synonymous and interchangeable. Seeking unity with God, or, rather, unity in the light or glory of God's presence, is the ultimate goal of every religion and spiritual philosophy. The Old Testament contains marvellous descriptions of this yearning:

> As a deer yearns
>   for running streams,
> so I yearn
>   for you, my God.
>
> I thirst for God,
>   the living God;
> when shall I go to see
>   the face of God?

I have no food but tears
    day and night,
as all day long I am taunted,
    'Where is your God?'

This I remember
    as I pour out my heart,
how I used to pass under the roof of the Most High,
    used to go to the house of God,
among cries of joy and praise,
    the sound of the feast.

Why be so downcast,
    why all these sighs?
Hope in God! I will praise him still,
    my Saviour, my God.

PSALM 42 *J*

Having established the fundamental law of the Creation, Psalm 24 gives hope and encouragement to those of us whose hands are not quite as clean as they might be. It refers to gates and doors, highly symbolic terms, and encourages us to 'lift up our heads' so as to open ourselves to let in the King of Glory, who is the Lord of Hosts. Many understand this to be the 'spirit', the soul of the soul, referred to in the first Beatitude. It is that part of us which is divine.

The reference by Jesus to Psalm 24 is riveting. The reading of the Beatitudes in these reflections has indicated that Jesus was teaching a foundation whereby all activities of life are related to the law given by God to Moses and the prophets. This is something far more profound than 'living a good life in an imperfect world' or endless days of trying to be virtuous. His is the way of perfection, 'I am the Way, the Truth and the Life'. It is the way of perfecting the whole of creation, not just our own existence in it.

In the Beatitudes, St Matthew has ordered the aphorisms to show, firstly, what we might now call the 'economic rules' that must be established, and, secondly, the qualities which human beings must develop both within themselves and in their relationships one to another. It might be called a conscious evolution, but not towards some collective of separate individual interests. It is not a 'spiritual communism'. It seems to be a progression towards unity in which individual interests become quiescent or even dormant. It perhaps has much in common with the early days of being in love: being at one's best for the sake of the beloved.

The yearning for this state is deep within us:

> If, however, from there you start searching once more for Yahweh your God, and if you search for him honestly and sincerely, you will find him. You will suffer; everything I have said will befall you, but in the final days you will return to Yahweh your God and listen to his voice. For Yahweh your God is a merciful God and will not desert or destroy you or forget the covenant which he made on oath with your ancestors.
>
> DEUTERONOMY 4 *J*

Even in the 1980s when the pursuit of individual interests was politically fashionable, an uneasiness troubled many in Western society. Today public examples of corporate greed trouble even more. Possessives such as 'mine' are not to be found in a pure heart. On the contrary, possessions tend to fill the heart, leaving little or no space for the light or glory of God. In this analysis we can see that the 'rich man' condemned by Jesus is rich not just because he has great wealth, but because in his heart he has many desires for great wealth. He wants it and he wants to possess it.

This is why a sharp line is drawn by Jesus between heaven and hell in the story of Lazarus (Luke 16). We are bound to suffer until we have purged ourselves of greed and selfishness, even when such selfishness extends to those close to us. The promise of blessedness, joy and happiness given by Jesus is to those who have abandoned their possessiveness. Suffering is for those of us who hold on.

But why should suffering be part of a process of seeking God? The Greek word for 'pure' in this Beatitude means purged of falsehood or free from impurities. Someone who is 'pure in heart' will have undergone a process which has cleansed them. Sometimes such processes are unlooked for and may manifest in dramatic, even devastating, occurrences.

Prayers of the heart, contemplation, or a system of meditation which displaces imagined creativity with a process of renouncing dreams, are to be found within the Christian tradition. They are practices which encourage the holding of a prayer, an idea or a mantra in the mind and in the heart, letting go of anything else which gets in the way. Any pain which might manifest from these practices arises from not letting go. This meditation is quite distinct from other practices which encourage the displacement of negative feelings with the creation of positive feelings.

The process of letting go in preference to acquiring more would make for a strange economy. It is a question for reflection as to which kind of society we prefer. Both societies are explored in the Psalms:

Not to us, Yahweh, not to us,
but to your name give the glory,
for your faithful love and your constancy!
Why should the nations ask, 'Where is their God?'

Our God is in heaven,
he creates whatever he chooses.
They have idols of silver and gold,
made by human hands.

These have mouths but say nothing,
have eyes but see nothing,
have ears but hear nothing,
have noses but smell nothing.

They have hands but cannot feel,
have feet but cannot walk,
no sound comes from their throats.
Their makers will end up like them,
everyone who relies on them.

PSALM 115 J

Yahweh is merciful and upright,
    our God is tenderness.
Yahweh looks after the simple,
    when I was brought low he gave me strength.

My heart, be at peace once again,
    for Yahweh has treated you generously.
He has rescued me from death, my eyes from tears,
    and my feet from stumbling.
I shall pass my life in the presence of Yahweh,
    in the land of the living.

PSALM 116 *J*

This Beatitude raises a vital question. Can we ever be free of selfishness in a world in which possessiveness is so strong? It is rather like asking whether we can dwell in the kingdom of heaven while living on earth. This might have been the question troubling the poet of this psalm while regarding the 'prosperity of the wicked':

Indeed God is good to Israel,
the Lord to those who are pure of heart.
My feet were on the point of stumbling;
a little more and I had slipped,
envying the arrogant as I did,
and seeing the prosperity of the wicked.
For them no such thing as pain,
untroubled, their comfortable portliness;
exempt from the cares which are the human lot,
they have no part in Adam's afflictions ...
Their mouth claims heaven for themselves,
and their tongue is never still on earth ...

That is why my people turn to them,
and enjoy the waters of plenty,
saying, 'How can God know?
What knowledge can the Most high have?
That is what the wicked are like,
piling up wealth without any worries …

Truly those who abandon you will perish;
you destroy those who adulterously desert you,
whereas my happiness is to be near God.
I have made the Lord Yahweh my refuge,
to tell of all your works.

PSALM 73 *J*

CHAPTER 7

The Peacemakers

*Blessed are the Peacemakers: for they shall be
called the children of God.*
AUTHORIZED VERSION

*Blessed are the peacemakers: they shall be
recognised as the children of God.*
NEW JERUSALEM BIBLE

*O the bliss of those who produce right relationships
between man and man,
for they are doing a God-like work!*
DAILY STUDY BIBLE

You're blessed when you can show people how
to cooperate instead of compete or fight.
That's when you discover who you really are,
and your place in God's family.

THE MESSAGE BIBLE

God blesses those people who make peace.
They will be called his children!

CONTEMPORARY ENGLISH VERSION

Blessed are those who plant peace each season;
they shall be named the children of God.

PRAYERS OF THE COSMOS

At first sight, this Beatitude is the most approachable. Peacemaking is a much respected activity and being called the children of God surely could not do any harm. Indeed, the Beatitude has something in common with the Hindu and Buddhist doctrine of *ahimsa* which means living in a way which does not cause harm to anyone or anything. The practice of ahimsa requires and induces a pure and merciful heart, and a frugal, simple and 'poor' way of life. Ahimsa sounds difficult but is reasonably straight-forward. In fact it requires the greatest wisdom and insight: ahimsa is not just a good intention. It requires you to know that your actions will not cause harm. Actions which inadvertently cause harm are not ahimsa. It is likely that Jesus did practise this discipline, for much of his teaching instructs his disciples in the way of harmlessness and it is thought by many that Jesus was a member of a Jewish sect called the Nazoreans, who were vegetarians. (They also held to the Mosaic doctrine of land distribution.)

Peace, whether it be peace between nations, people or families, or peace within ourselves, our hearts, minds and bodies, is rare and often difficult to find. Certainly it eluded the Israelites, despite the urgings of their prophets who maintained that peace would come from the practice of justice and virtue:

> Fair judgement will fix its home in the desert,
> and uprightness live in the productive ground,
> and the product of uprightness will be peace,
> the effect of uprightness being quiet and security
>   for ever.
>
> Many people will live in a peaceful home,
> in peaceful houses, tranquil dwellings.
> And should the forest be totally destroyed
> and the city gravely humiliated,
> you will be happy to sow wherever there is water
> and to let the ox and the donkey roam free.

ISAIAH 32 J

Yet the Peacemaker Beatitude is not quite what it seems and in many ways this text is the most obscure. The word 'peacemakers' is not used elsewhere in the Bible. It is hardly to be found in 'classical' Greek. Therefore it is not possible to refer to an exact Old Testament text to confirm its meaning. However, the idea of 'peace' is understood by Christians to be an essential element of their message. According to St Luke, John the Baptist, who is the bridge between the Old and the New, was greeted by his father Zechariah with this prophesy:

> And you, little child,
> you shall be called Prophet of the Most High,
> For you will go before the Lord
> to prepare a way for him,
> to give his people knowledge of salvation
> through the forgiveness of their sins,
> because of the faithful love of our God
> in which the rising Sun has come from on high
> to visit us,
> to give light to those who live
> in darkness and the shadow dark as death,
> and to guide our feet
> into the way of peace.
>
> St Luke 1 J

John's mission to affirm the 'way of peace' was confirmed upon Jesus when a dove, the symbol of peace, descended on him while being baptized. Peace was understood to be in the nature of the heavenly rule. At

Christmas, St Luke's welcome to the baby Jesus is read throughout Christendom:

> For unto you is born this day in the city of David a saviour, which is Christ the Lord.
>
> And this shall be a sign unto you; Ye shall find the babe wrapped in swaddling clothes lying in a manger.
>
> And suddenly there was with the angel a multitude of the heavenly host praising God, and saying,
>
> Glory to God in the highest and on earth, peace and goodwill towards men.
>
> LUKE 2 *AV*

The Authorized Version offers peace openly and generously 'towards men'. Modern scholars find qualifications:

> Glory to God in highest heaven
> And on earth his peace for men on whom his favour rests.
>
> NEW ENGLISH BIBLE

> Glory to God in the highest heaven,
> and on earth peace for those he favours.
>
> NEW JERUSALEM BIBLE

> Glory to God in the heavenly heights,
> Peace to all men and women on earth who please him.
>
> THE MESSAGE BIBLE

Praise God in Heaven,
Peace on earth to everyone who pleases God.

CONTEMPORARY ENGLISH VERSION

These are not quite the same as the Authorized Version! And, of course, 'pleasing God' is not the highest item on most people's lists as they enter the Christmas festivities!

St Luke establishes from the outset that Jesus has come to fulfil the utterances of the prophets. Here, in magnificent language, is another Nativity reading:

> The people that walked in darkness have seen a great light: they that dwell in the land of the shadow of death, upon them hath the light shined ...

> For unto us a child is born, unto us a child is given: and the government shall be upon his shoulder: and his name shall be called Wonderful, Counsellor, The mighty God, The everlasting Father, The Prince of Peace.

> Of the increase of his government there shall be no end, upon the throne of David ... and to establish it with judgement and with justice from henceforth even for ever. The zeal of the Lord of hosts will perform this.

ISAIAH 9 AV

Later, Isaiah eliminates those who will not receive peace:

> I create the fruit of the lips; Peace, peace to him that is far off, and to him that is near, saith the Lord; and I will heal him.

But the wicked are like the troubled sea, when it cannot rest, whose waters cast up mire and dirt.

There is no peace, saith my God, to the wicked.

ISAIAH 57 *AV*

Denial of peace to the wicked in favour of those who please God is refined by Jesus. When instructing his disciples to proclaim the kingdom of Heaven to the Jews in the towns and villages of Palestine, he suggests they find someone 'worthy' to stay with:

As you enter his house, salute it, and if the house deserves it, may your peace come upon it; if it does not, may your peace come back to you.

MATTHEW 10 *J*

And in the same speech, Jesus makes one of those statements which Christians find hard to resolve:

Do not suppose that I have come to bring peace to the earth: it is not peace I have come to bring, but a sword. For I have come to set son against father, daughter against mother, daughter-in-law against mother-in-law; a person's enemies will be the members of his own household.

MATTHEW 10 *J*

In the rabbinical tradition it was held that at 'the end of days', the time of judgement, families would divide against one another. In quoting this idea Jesus strongly identifies himself with the rabbinical tradition. Is he using words like peace and sword to define a role or infer a meaning no longer available to us? In St John's Gospel we find Jesus in dialogue with the disciples saying:

> Peace I bequeath to you,
> my own peace I give you,
> a peace which the world cannot give, this is my gift
> to you.
> Do not let your hearts be troubled or afraid.
>
> JOHN 14 J

'Blessed are the peacemakers' infers that peace is somehow made or created. Yet in the passage from St John, as in some others, peace appears to be a gift, a transference from God to the earth or mankind, or from one person to another. Before looking at what peace might be it might be helpful to examine the promise which Jesus makes – 'to be called the children of God'.

The precise phrase 'children of God' is also rare; it ocurrs just three times in the Gospels and not at all in the Old Testament. In St Luke, Jesus has been asked a tricky question about a woman who has been legally married to seven men. In the 'after life', who would be her husband? In his perceptive answer, Jesus makes reference to the children of God:

> … for they are the same as angels, and being children
> of the resurrection they are the children of God.
>
> LUKE 20 J

According to William Barclay, the Greek word which has been translated as 'children' is more accurately translated as 'sons', thus:

... they shall be called the sons of God.

This is a highly significant title in the Jewish tradition. Originally it was used in a legend to describe unholy marriages between the daughters of the Israelites and a race of 'supermen':

> When people began being numerous on earth, and daughters had been born to them, the sons of God, looking at the women saw how beautiful they were and married as many as they chose.
>
> GENESIS 6 J

Later, 'sons of God' was used to desribe angels. The word 'angel' means messenger. Some angels were guardians while others were destroying angels. In Job we read that:

> One day when the sons of God came to attend on Yahweh, among them came Satan. So Yahweh said to Satan, 'Where have you been?' 'Prowling around on earth,' he answered. 'Roaming around there.'
>
> JOB 1 J

At that time, Satan was seen more as a tempter, a Iago, rather than the Evil One of Christianity. In a Job text quoted in 'Blessed are the Meek ...', we read of 'sons of God' praising the extent of the phenomenal world:

> Who laid its cornerstone
> to the joyful acclaim of the sons of God?

Being that the establishment of peace, either within oneself or in society or between nations, is so hard, it is not suprising that Jesus would wish to call such miracle workers 'angels'. But the problem for this series of reflections is that it doesn't quite fit the underlying sequence. There is yet another possiblity.

The prophet Hosea was well known to Jesus, who quoted him in Luke. Hosea sees Israel as a faithless wife who is won back, having been tested by her husband. The husband is thought to be a symbol for God and the wife for Israel. But at this time there was also another terrible schism between the tribes of Judah and Israel. And just as this was a time of dissension, so in Jerusalem in the lifetime of Jesus there was considerable friction. There were over 24 different schools of Jewish thought in Jerusalem alone, many mutually antagonistic, and all weakening the Jewish cause. They eagerly awaited a Messiah who, as 'a single head', would unite them. At the beginning of his Book, Hosea makes a prediction:

> They will be told they are 'Children of the living God'.
>
> The Judaens and Israelites will be reunited
> and will choose themselves a single head,
> and will spread far beyond their country,
> for great will be the Day of Jezreel!
> Then call your brothers, 'My people',
> and your sisters, 'You have been pitied'.*

HOSEA 2 J

* In the Hebrew Bible this is better translated as 'lovingly accepted'.

In the account of events leading up to the Jewish Passover in St John's Gospel, the fate of Jesus was being discussed by the senior rabbis and priests:

> One of them, Caiaphas, the high priest that year, said, 'You do not seem to have grasped the situation at all; you fail to see that it is to your advantage that one man should die for the people, rather than that the whole nation should perish.' He did not speak in his own person, but as high priest of that year he was prophesying that Jesus was to die for the nation – and not for the nation only, but also to gather together into one the scattered children of God.
>
> JOHN 11 J

It seems certain that Jesus, St John, and the priest Caiaphas were all aware of the Hosean prophecy and that Jesus and Caiaphas wanted reunification of the Jewish nation. Anyone who could bring peace and unification to a society based upon love and forgiveness, a society purged of selfishness and greed and which based its conduct on God-given laws, would be little lower than an angel.

The question might be put: 'How could such a society come about without peace – a very deep peace, perhaps "the peace of God which passeth all understanding" – being communicated into the heart of the community?' Only by having recourse to the constant presence of this God-given peace could the pillars of the Beatitudes be realized:

God is our refuge and strength, a very present help in trouble.

Therefore will not we fear, though the earth be removed, and though the mountains be carried into the midst of the sea;

Though the waters thereof roar and be troubled, though the mountains shake with the swelling thereof. Selah.

There is a river, the streams whereof shall make glad the city of God, the holy place of the tabernacles of the most High.

God is in the midst of her; she shall not be moved: God shall help her and that right early.

The heathen raged, the kingdoms were moved: he uttered his voice, the earth melted.

The Lord of hosts is with us; the God of Jacob is our refuge. Selah.

Come, behold the works of the Lord, what desolations he hath made in the earth.

He maketh wars to cease unto the end of the earth; he breaketh the bow, and cutteth the spear in sunder; he burneth the chariot in the fire.

Be still and know that I am God: I will be exulted among the heathen, I will be exalted in the earth.

The Lord of hosts is with us; the God of Jacob is our refuge. Selah.

PSALM 46 *AV*

'Be still and know I am God' is the basis of the practice of ahimsa. For it is only when still that the mind can hear 'the still small voice' which guides thoughts, feelings and actions. But how to be still? A simple question. It has much in common with finding 'a pure heart'. Perhaps just as to find purity we need to let go of the impure, so stillness is discovered when we let go of agitation and noise. It is a letting go of our personal claim on the world.

CHAPTER 8

The Persecuted

*Blessed are they which are persecuted for
righteousness' sake:
for theirs is the kingdom of heaven.*
AUTHORIZED VERSION

*Blessed are those who are persecuted in the cause
of uprightness:
the kingdom of Heaven is theirs.*
NEW JERUSALEM BIBLE

*The bliss of the sufferer for Christ.
The bliss of the blood-stained way.*
DAILY STUDY BIBLE

*You're blessed when you can show people how to
cooperate instead of compete or fight.
The persecution drives you even deeper into
God's kingdom.*
THE MESSAGE BIBLE

*God blesses those people who are treated badly
for doing right.
They belong to the kingdom of heaven.*
CONTEMPORARY ENGLISH VERSION

*Tuned to the Source are those persecuted
for trying to right society's balance:
to them belongs the coming king- and queendom*
PRAYERS OF THE COSMOS

*I*t is rather surprising to discover that the word
'persecuted' is not frequently used in the Bible.
It is surprising because, from the historical point of
view, the Bible records a great deal of persecution.
Throughout the history of the 'People of The One God',

Jews, Christians and Moslems have all been persecuted and have all been rather good at persecution, from the earliest times to now. In his book about St Matthew, William Barclay describes how the Christians suffered under the Roman Emperor Nero:

> All the world knows of the Christians who were flung to the lions or burned at the stake; but these were kindly deaths. Nero wrapped the Christians in pitch and set them alight, and used them as living torches to light his gardens. He sewed them in the skins of wild animals and set his hunting dogs upon them to tear them to death. They were tortured on the rack; they were scraped with pincers; molten lead was poured hissing upon them; red hot brass plates were affixed to the tenderest parts of their bodies; eyes were torn out; parts of their bodies were cut off and roasted before their eyes; their hands and feet were burned while cold water was poured over them to lengthen the agony. These things are not pleasant to think about, but these are the things a man had to be prepared for, if he took his stand with Christ.
>
> DAILY STUDY BIBLE

In the 15th century, the Catholics, led by Ferdinand and Isabella, regained control of Spain from the Moslems. To purge the population of what they believed to be the twin 'evils' of Islam and Judaism, they devised the Inquisition. Anyone considered to be a Jew, a Moslem, or a Christian who rejected the concept of the Holy Trinity, was burned slowly over a fire, ideally for an hour or so, before dying. The screams were not thought to be the victim's. They were screams of 'escaping devils' who were finding the body of the victim too painful for further occupancy. The victim would be comforted by the thought that after having been purged in this way, he would be offered a place in 'Heaven'. The time when these events took place followed a period of history when Moslems, Christians and Jews had worked closely together in Spain to create a shining and caring culture, which then permeated the whole of Europe.

At the time of Jesus, Rome persecuted mercilessly anyone who disturbed the 'pax Romana', the peace of Rome, especially if that disturbance presented a challenge to her authority, which that created by the Jews of Palestine certainly did. And there is plenty of evidence to suggest that Jesus was well aware of his impending crucifixion. Indeed, he expected it. His cries of 'My God, my God, why hast thou foresaken me', were the fulfilment of Isaiah's prophesies and the Psalms:

> My God, my God, why have you forsaken me?
> The words of my groaning do nothing to save me.
> My God, I call by day but you do not answer,
> at night, but I find no response ...

> PSALM 22 J

This psalm continues by describing the dreadful plight of the psalmist which foreshadowed the events of the crucifixion:

> I can count every one of my bones,
> while they look on and gloat;
> they divide my garments among them
> and cast lots for my clothing.

Following a further plea for God's help, the psalmist begins a paeon of praise, prophesying the return of all people to the unity of God:

> The whole wide world will remember and return to
>   Yahweh,
> all the families of the nations bow down before him.
> For to Yahweh, ruler of the nations, belongs kingly
>   power!
> All who prosper on earth will bow down before him,
> and who go down to the dust will do reverence
>   before him.
> And those who are dead, their descendants will serve
>   him,
> will proclaim his name to generations still to come;
> and these will tell of his saving justice to a people yet
>   unborn.

PSALM 22 *J*

Whether we take the view that Jesus was the Messiah or Christ, the Son of God come to redeem the world from sin, the prophecies still had to be fulfilled. Suffering had to be endured – it was written in the scripture. But why did Jesus say that the persecuted *are* happy and joyful? For, as in the first Beatitude, the promise is not for a heavenly future. They *are* blessed now; '… for theirs *is* the kingdom of heaven' means that it is present here and now, in the midst of persecution, not after it is all over or before it has begun.

Before exploring further, it is worth considering whether this was a Beatitude given by Jesus within this series. Following on from the Beatitude, St Matthew's text states:

> Blessed are you when people abuse you and persecute you and speak all manner of calumny against you on my account. Rejoice and be glad, for your reward *will be* great in heaven; this is how they persecuted the prophets before you.

> MATTHEW 5 J

The italics are used here to emphasize one of the differences between these very similar texts; the Beatitude is concerned with the present while the verse promises something in the future. Could it be that some early scribe, or even Matthew himself, invented the eighth Beatitude? The number seven and its multiples are to be found throughout St Matthew as a way of ordering text. The Lord's Prayer is an example. The number has a mystical significance; decimalized it becomes a numeric sequence which repeats until the end of time! Seven Beatitudes would accord with Matthew's system, eight would not.

On the other hand, the Beatitude is strengthened by the fact that the Gospels in Greek, and subsequently Latin, were not ordered into numbered sentences until the 13th century. So it is possible that, given the enormous amount of biblical text, some errors have been made.

A different kind of problem is that the Authorized Version uses the word 'persecute' or 'persecuted' in preference to a wide variety of words and expressions chosen by contemporary scholars. They do use the word 'persecuted', but more often 'slaughter without pity', 'furiously lashing', 'hate and hated me', 'confound', 'pursue', 'hound', 'drive them away', and 'root them out' are found.

Of course, the translators of the Authorized Version were only too aware of persecution. Men like Tyndale and Cranmer had been recently executed. Religious dissent was sweeping through England and the authorities persecuted 'dissenters' ruthlessly. The scholars and bishops working on the new English language Bible would have been well aware of their precarious position. For them, the experience of religious life would have included persecution, so they may have overworked the word.

The Old Testament uses the word 'persecute' or 'persecuted' when the Israelites are praying to God to attack their enemies:

Let them be as chaff before the wind: and let the angel of the Lord chase them.

Let their way be dark and slippery, and let the angel of the Lord persecute them …

Let destruction come upon him at unawares ... into that very destruction let him fall.

And my soul shall be joyful in the Lord ...

PSALM 35 *AV*

The word is also used to describe how God takes his vengeance upon the wicked, in this case the King of Babylon:

How did the tyrant end?
How did his arrogance end?

Yahweh has broken the staff of the wicked,
the sceptre of rulers
furiously lashing* peoples
with continual blows,
angrily hammering nations,
pursuing without respite.

ISAIAH 14 *J*

* 'Persecuted' in *AV*.

Again, 'persecuted' is used to describe God taking vengeance upon the Israelites:

Let us search and try our ways, and turn again to the Lord.

Let us lift up our heart with our hands unto our God in the heavens.

We have transgressed and have rebelled: thou hast not pardoned.

Thou hast covered with anger, and persecuted us:
thou hast slain, thou hast not pitied.

Thou hast covered thyself with a cloud, that our
prayer should not pass through.

LAMENTATIONS 3 *AV*

The word 'persecution' is rarely used in the Gospels.
Jesus predicts that the missionaries of the early church
will suffer by it:

Brother will betray brother to death, and a father his
child; children will come forward against their parents
and have them put to death. You will be universally
hated on account of my name; but anyone who stands
firm to the end will be saved. If they persecute you in
one town, take refuge in the next; and if they persecute you in that, take refuge in another.

MATTHEW 10 *J*

And again Matthew uses the word in the passage which
foretells the destruction of the Temple in Jerusalem:

Wherefore, behold, I send unto you prophets, and
wise men, and scribes: and some of them ye shall
kill and crucify; and some of them ye shall scourge
in your synagogues, and persecute them from city
to city:

MATTHEW 23 *AV*

In St John, Jesus gives some kind of explanation why
people are persecuted:

If the world hates you,
you must realise that it hated me before it hated you.

If you belonged to the world,
the world would love you as its own;
but because you do not belong to the world,
because my choice of you has drawn you out of the
world,
that is why the world hates you.

JOHN 15 J

Why should the world 'hate' Jesus? – the man whose
message to the world is 'love one another'. It is a big
question and certainly a big hatred. Jesus the teacher
reminded people of the law, a law declared to Moses
and given by God to the Israelites for the benefit of all
humanity.

This law often conflicts with individual interests
and, at times, with common interests. However, many
believed that their very existence depended on the
maintenance of these interests, and thus the ruling
Jewish priesthood, the Sadduccees and the Romans,
persecuted Jesus and his followers.

The Mosaic law required people to let go – to let go
of possessions of every kind. In the end they might be
asked to let go of life itself. This was something which
the early Christians did gladly. Not 'My will to live', but
'Thy will be done on earth'.

Yet none of this clarifies why Jesus and St Matthew
should present persecution as the final glory of the
Beatitudes. What could there be in the Jewish consciousness at that time which would lead Jesus' disciples
to cry out with acclaim at the mention of persecution?

We will never know for sure, but there is an example of persecution in the Old Testament which corresponds not just to the historical events of Jesus' time, but also to the essence of what Jesus was asking for.

In the Second Book of Maccabees we read of a true story of persecution and incredible endurance, virtue and love which occurred some 150 years before the birth of Jesus. It was at a time when great profanities were taking place in the Temple, and when the law was being ignored by Jews and Gentiles alike. It was a time for the 'godfearing' to take a stand.

A woman and her seven sons were arrested by the king and told to eat pork, something forbidden by the law. They refused, preferring torture to breaking the laws of their ancestors. The king became furious and ordered pans and cauldrons to be heated. The eldest son's tongue was cut out, he was scalped, and his 'extremities were cut off'. He was then fried on a red hot pan in front of his mother and brothers. Pork was then offered to the second brother and again it was refused. And so, one by one, the family was tortured to death.

This story had so much power that centuries later churches were still being dedicated to the memory of the Passion of the Holy Maccabees, and Christian martyrs perished with their names on their lips. The Jews of Palestine knew the story well, so if Jesus was referring to it in this Beatitude, it would have been to strengthen the resolve of his followers to live the law. It would also remind them that from time to time there is a need to let go of life itself for a greater cause. Letting go of what we hold most dear can transform events.

Whilst a prisoner of war, Laurens van der Post was ordered to stand in a queue of soldiers to be beaten, one by one, across head and shoulders with a chair. Having picked himself up off the ground, he stepped forward for another beating. This so upset the soldiers' sense of routine that they stopped, glared at him and then stormed off, leaving many men unharmed. Most of us hang on to what life is offering us, even when life is miserable. To let go of everything for the sake of the great causes of Justice and Mercy is to show the love which Jesus commanded and exemplified.

Epilogue

When I began the research for this book I expected to be writing about the Beatitudes as 'steps on the ladder of spiritual consciousness' or 'the secret language of the kingdom'! And I would have been quite right to be doing so. The Beatitudes encompass all of these. But to be led towards ancient systems of Jewish land tenure, usury and the challenge of poverty set against an ever-increasing desire for wealth was a surprise. It was also a delight. It began to shift a view I had somehow acquired that Christianity was all to do with building a better tomorrow; that salvation from sin would lead to my future eternal life in heaven. I had come to believe that heaven would offer a pleasant and comfortable existence.

I have always had difficulty in imagining that there is any work to be done in heaven. I have thought of it as ordered, with garden weeds knowing their rightful place, and mice who do not eat springtime bulbs. No drains to be unblocked or roofs to be repaired. But as reading, research and reflection on the Beatitudes proceeded, I began to think that if these vague notions had any place in the cosmic scheme of things, they would belong to something Jesus called the 'afterlife', and that heaven and hell belong here on earth.

A heavenly future in which all things will be perfected has been a most useful device for persuading humanity to serve the vested interests of the day. 'Things take time to build,' we say, and in a world of future promise they never stop taking time. In the 1970s 'futurists' wrote about how we would live at the beginning of the new millennium. Robots and computers were going to cause a crisis of leisure. Work would be so 'automated' that most of us would be freed from daily drudgery and it was seriously suggested that we could expect four days of freedom each week to spend as we will.

Today, another generation promises a new technology to bring benefits to humankind. All eyes continue to look to the future, to an improved future: one which has been 'tempered by the mistakes of the past'. Humanity has always found the future compelling, and in our minds we remain subject to its allure. If we try to find a moment to sit down and gently bring the mind to rest on a biblical text, what do we find? A phone call to be made, clothes to be ironed, a window to be opened, a door to be closed, a note to be made for the following day. The more time spent looking forward, the less time available for the present. There is an immense pressure of thought stealing our attention.

And so it is with the communal world at large, which mirrors our minds and our hearts. Future growth is all important and we are told a growing economy is a sure sign of a prosperous future. Our expectation of a growing economy requires a relentless increase in wealth. Having become a little uneasy about the viability of such a prospect, top executives and perceptive managers divide their corporations into smaller units so as to encourage regrowth from a lower base. There is a strong belief that if organizations, national governments or individuals, come to rest, they will fail.

One of the reasons for this anticipation of failure is the mountain of debt which is accumulating in the world. This debt needs servicing by payment of usury, or 'interest' as it is politely called. As we have seen, Jesus does not ransom the future. He forbids the levy of interest and he encourages his followers to make loans to those in need without thought of repayment. Payment of interest and repayment of debt can only be made in the future if enough wealth is created in the future to do so. If there is insufficient wealth, standards of living decline. Politicians will tell us to 'tighten our belts' and work harder to create more wealth, which in our system creates more debt.

Traditionally, when indebtebdness becomes excessive, children have often been sold into slavery. Those concerned with lending will always secure their title to land. Lenders have always hedged their bets, and even today in the United Kingdom, the favoured way to secure a loan is by title to land. The system declared by Moses and the prophets, and revived by Jesus, to return people to their land in the year of the jubilee was devised to ensure people were not enslaved. They were given a breathing space to recover from adversity and a chance to begin anew with their ancient allotments, and lenders were made to forfeit all claims.

Throughout the 20th century a perceived struggle between the 'haves and the have nots' has dominated ideology. This has obscured the endless and underlying conflict between those who love truth, justice and mercy, and those who manipulate ignorance to protect their vested interests. It was to find freedom from such powerful interests that the Pilgrim Fathers and many other Europeans voyaged to the open and free space of America. But today these vested interests continue, not only by accumulating wealth from the poorer nations, but also by pillaging the third world cultures of wisdom in order to help buttress the very system which impoverishes them. Meditation techniques now are often recommended to employees, not to enable truth to be realized but as an aid to increased production!

Usurous capitalism has shown great resilience and adaptability. It has proved itself to be a survivor, supported by the tradition of civil freedom in Western countries. But in recent years it has become concerned with 'my' world and 'my' prosperity and 'my' incentive for a better life. It is like the 'rich' man in the Lazarus story. We no longer conceive of a way of salvation for all of humanity or for the world of which we are stewards. The teachings of Jesus are concerned with the greater good of all, but are in constant danger of succumbing to degenerate cultural ideas.

Two thousand years ago, Palestine was experiencing extreme degeneration. And then one man, maybe a sagacious Jew, maybe the Messiah, but to the minds of countless millions, Jesus the Christ, Son of God, brought a message of renewal: a living law originally given by God to Moses. Jesus added a simple message of three words: 'Love one another'. In the Beatitudes he set out the principles of a simple scheme of universal salvation. It offers freedom and justice to everyone now. Not 'Blessed were' or 'Blessed will be' but 'Blessed'!

These reflections on the Beatitudes raise some very difficult issues, both at personal and communal levels. What if we think ourselves rich or if we own more land than we can manage or need? And if we are in the business of lending money, how should we deal with unpaid debt? A community based on the Beatitudes would restore simplicity to everyday life. If this were taken up universally I doubt that the Amazon rainforest would be under threat or that poisons would be polluting the air and disturbing the climate.

St Francis of Assisi made heroic efforts to realize the teaching of Jesus. And in this century, Mahatma Gandhi and Vinobe Bhave have also attempted to bring together principles of economy and spirituality. And in his book *No Destination* Satish Kumar writes of the hard struggles to transfer just small amounts of land to the landless poor. The harmony between the teachings of Jesus, St Francis and Mahatma Gandhi makes any differences pale into insignificance.

The Beatitudes challenge the economies and economic theories developed by the all-powerful secular economists of the past 200 years. They guide us on how to live together in freedom. In places like Qumran, Christians and Jews tried to put these principles into practice, as have many other groups over the centuries.

The Beatitudes are like the pillars of a Gothic cathedral. They connect the soaring roof, indicator of infinite spirit, to the firm ground on which we all stand. In the space between, the kingdom of heaven is ever present. As William Blake observed in 'Auguries of Innocence':

> To see a World in a Grain of Sand,
> And a Heaven in a Wild Flower,
> Hold Infinity in the palm of your hand,
> And Eternity in an hour.

The pillars hold the structure, they are the markers, but they raise problems and questions. To answer these we need bibles, a concordance and the practice of reflection. The teaching of love and harmlessness, embodied in the Sermon on the Mount require deep and resolute application. I have a feeling that there is quite a lot of work to be done in heaven.

Reflection and Meditation

There is a growing interest in spiritual practices. In the 1960s, Maharishi Mahesh Yogi brought an Indian system of meditation to the West and he was followed by a succession of spiritual teachers bringing with them a variety of practices. This prompted a response within the Christian tradition which hitherto had rather lost its way in this regard, except in some monastic orders, parts of the Orthodox Church, and in places where the practice of Gregorian and plainsong chant was continued. Formerly, Christianity had been rich in spiritual practice – something evident in books such as *The Cloud of Unknowing*, *The Imitation of Christ*, and the writings of Meister Eckhart. In 1975, Dom John Main opened the first Christian Meditation Centre in London, which was formalized as an international movement at a seminar in Indiana in 1991.

A wide range of spiritual practices, representing religious and other traditions, including prayer, meditation, contemplation, reflection and chanting, are now available for those who seek them. All these practices contribute to a spiritual way of life but differ both in purpose and the response they engender in our being. While many books on this subject are available, it must be stressed that for those interested in spiritual practice there is no substitute for personal guidance from someone who is trustworthy, experienced, and who 'practices what they preach'! Anyone seeking to develop spiritually must be prepared to give care and time to their exploration.

The word 'meditation' may be used in two ways. It may be used to describe a series of reflective thoughts such as in *The Meditations of Marcus Aurelius*. But in spiritual practice its meaning is more precise. Meditation is concerned with the repetition of a word, in Eastern traditions it is called a 'mantra; in Christian meditation a 'pure prayer'. This word enables us to transcend physical sensations, and mental and emotional agitation so that we experience the spiritual or divine dimension within us. It leads us beyond the familiar world where sensations, feelings and ideas come and go. During a period of meditation, the body and mind may experience stillness and deep peace. On the other hand, they may not. If, like the author, you find the experience of the second condition more familiar, do not be deterred. Meditation is a practice and it may well be that the fruits of the practice of meditation manifest at other times. What is important during the practice is to free the attention from any thought and sensations which arise, and to bring it back to the word or phrase being repeated. The practice of meditation is not concerned with imagining anything. Rather, it is to permit the word to lead us to the still centre of our being, letting go of any distractions which may arise on the way. Most difficulties arise from wanting immediate results.

Reflection also requires practice and physical stillness; it requires the mind to come to rest on a concept, idea or image so that the qualities of mind work to discriminate between truth and falsehood. It is a simple exercise which does not require high intellectual ability or special qualifications. The mind will offer a great deal of ideas, thoughts and even sensations in response to the subject in mind. The process is to let go of what is experienced and to return one's attention to the subject in question. Again, gentle patience is practised. The incoming ideas may become refined and something may arise which is recognized as being of special significance by the way it illuminates the mind as well as the subject being considered.

In meditation and reflection, the underlying process is to let go of what the mind constantly produces: the mind has a seemingly infinite ability to produce ideas.

Practice soon reveals the general agitated state of our minds and emotions, which is reflected in the larger world of human experience. It may also show us how we have been conditioned to analyze things until they become separate from the unity of which all things are part. While these things may have weakened our inner intuitive knowledge we should never be discouraged by their presence. Meditation and reflection will strengthen these aspects of our being. For guidance on general principals applicable to all religious and spiritual traditions, *Good Company*, by Shantanand Saraswati is highly recommended. Other meditative techniques which require the *creation* of inner mental and emotional states are not considered in this book.

Bibliography

Barclay, William, *Daily Study Bible*, Saint Andrew Press, Edinburgh, 1975

Berry, Wendell, *Standing on Earth; Selected Essays*, Golgonooza Press, Ipswich, 1991

Cloud of Unknowing, The, (introduced by Laurence Freeman), Element Books, Shaftesbury, 1996

Coomaraswamy, Ananda, *Volume 2: Selected Papers 'Metaphysics'*, Princetown University Press, New Jersey, 1977

Corstanje, Auspicius van, *The Covenant with God's Poor*, Franciscan Herald Press, Chicago, 1966

Crosby, Michael H, *Spirituality of the Beatitudes*, Orbis Books, Maryknoll, 1980

Cruden, Alexander, *Cruden's Complete Concordance to the Old and New Testaments*, Lutterworth Press, London, 1954

Douglas-Klotz, Neil, *Prayers of the Cosmos*, Harper Collins, New York, 1990

Eisenman, Robert, *The Dead Sea Scrolls and the First Christians*, Element Books, Shaftesbury, 1996

Geary, Frank, *Land Tenure and Unemployment*, George Allen & Unwin, London, 1925

George, Susan, *A Fate Worse than Debt*, Penguin, London, 1994

The Holy Bible, (Authorized King James Version), Oxford University Press, London

Jupp, Kenneth, *Jubilee 2000*, Land Policy Council, London, 1997

Jupp, Kenneth, *Stealing our Land, The Law, Rent and Taxation*, Vindex Press, London, 1997

Keating, Thomas, *Invitation to Love*, Element Books, Shaftesbury, 1992

Koshoo, T N, *Mahatma Gandhi: An Apostle of Peace*, Tata Energy Research Institute, New Delhi, 1995

Kumar, Satish, *No Destination*, Green Books, Totness, 1992

New Jerusalem Bible, Standard Edition, Darton, Longman & Todd, London, 1985

Peterson, Eugene H, *The Message*, NavPress Publishing Group, Colorado Springs, 1993

Prabhavananda, Swami, *The Sermon on the Mount According to Vedanta*, Vedanta Press, California, 1963

Contemporary English Version, Thomas Nelson Inc, Nashville, 1995

Schonfield, Hugh, *The Passover Plot*, Element Books, Shaftesbury, 1993

Selby, Peter, *Grace and Mortgage*, Darton, Longman & Todd, London, 1997

Sri Shantanand Saraswati, *Good Company*, Element Books, Shaftesbury, 1987

Thomas à Kempis, *The Imitation of Christ*, (available in numerous editions)

Walshe, M O'C (trans and ed), *Meister Eckhart: Sermons & Treatises* (3 Volumes), Element Books, Shaftesbury, 197AUSTRALIA

Meditation Centres

AUSTRALIA

**The Christian
Meditation Community**
PO Box 6630
St Kilda Road Central
Melbourne 3004

CANADA

**The Christian
Meditation Centre**
1283 Moffat Avenue
Quebec H4H121

NEW ZEALAND

**The Christian
Meditation Centre**
4 Argyle Road
Browns Bay
Auckland 1310

UNITED KINGDOM

The School of Meditation
158 Holland Park Avenue
London W11

**The World Community
for Christian Meditation**
23 Kensington Square
London W8 5HHN

USA

**The Christian
Meditation Center**
322 East 94th Street–4B
New York MY10128

**The Christian
Meditation Center**
1080 West Irving Park Road
Roselle
Illinois 60172

Index of First Lines

A

Again the kingdom of heaven is like a dragnet
    MATTHEW 13:47   19

Although affliction cometh not forth JOB 5:6   32

And he brought him forth abroad GENESIS 15:5   46

And in that day shall the deaf hear ISAIAH 29:18   40

And Issac called Jacob, and blessed him GENESIS 28:1   46

And Mary said, My soul doth magnify LUKE 1:46   83

And these are the countries JOSHUA 14:1   50

And they shall build the old wastes, ISAIAH 61:4   45

And you, little child, LUKE 1:76   100

As a deer yearns for running streams PSALM 42:1   89

As you enter his house, salute it MATTHEW 10:12   103

Ask, and it will be given to you MATTHEW 7:7   21

At the end of every seven years DEUTERONOMY 15:1   58, 79

B

Beatitudes MATTHEW 5:3, LUKE 6:20

Blessed are the poor in spirit MATTHEW 5:3   5

Blessed are you when people abuse you MATTHEW 5:11   116

Blessed be ye poor LUKE 6:20   5

Blessed is he that considereth the poor PSALM 41:1   xix

Better someone living an honest life PROVERBS 28:6   7

Brother will betray brother to death MATTHEW 10:21   119

But I say this to you who are listening LUKE 6:27   80

D

Do not be stubborn like your ancestors   2 Chronicles 30:8   75
Do not suppose that I have come   Matthew 10:34   103

F

Fair judgement will fix its home   Isaiah 33:16   99
For if ye forgive men their trespasses   Matthew 6:14   80
For look, I am going to create new heavens   Isaiah 65:1   41
... for they are the same as angels   Luke 20:36   104
For unto you is born this day   Luke 2:11   101

G

Gird thy sword upon thy thigh   Psalm 45:3   39
Glory to God in the highest heaven   Luke 2:14   101
God is our refuge and strength   Psalms 46:1   108

H

Have you ever in your life given orders   Job 38:12   51
He called the twelve together   Luke 9:1   17
He had no form or charm to attract us   Isaiah 53:2   40
He that putteth not out his money   Psalm 15:5   55
He then said, 'Please show me your ...'   Exodus 33:18   88
He ... went into the synagogue   Luke 4:16   64
Heal me, Yahweh, my bones are shaken   Psalm 6:2   12
Hear the word of the Lord ye children   Hosea 4:1   29
Hearken to me, ye that follow   Isaiah 51:1   61
Here we are, fools for Christ's sake   1 Corinthians 4   9
How deserted she sits   Lamentations 1:1   27
How did the tyrant end?   Isaiah 14:4   118
How hard it is for those who have riches   Luke 18:24   6
How long will the land be in mourning   Jeremiah 12:4   31

I

I can count everyone of my bones   Psalm 22:17   115
I create the fruit of the lips;   Isaiah 57:19   102

I looked to the earth JEREMIAH 4:23   26
I, wisdom share house with Discretion PROVERBS 8:12   62
If his will is to raise up the downcast JOB 5:11   33
If, however, from there you start searching
    DEUTERONOMY 4:29   91
If the world hates you, JOHN 15:18   119
If ye love me, keep my commandments JOHN 14:15   36
If you lend money to any of my people EXODUS 22:24   78
If your brother becomes impoverished LEVITICUS 25:35   78
In that case who can be saved? LUKE 18:26   6
In the beginning was the Word JOHN 1:1   87
Indeed God is good to Israel PSALM 73:1   94
Is there anyone poor among you, DEUTERONOMY 15:7   47, 57

J

Judges and officers shalt thou make thee DEUTERONOMY 16   50

K

Keep in mind your promise PSALM 119:49   34

L

Let them be as chaff before the wind PSALM 35:5   117
Let us search and try our ways LAMENTATIONS 3:40   118
Listen to this, you elders JOEL 1:1   27

M

Moses then gave the Israelites this order NUMBERS 34:13   49
My God, my God, why have you forsaken me?
    PSALM 22:1   10, 114

N

Not to us, Yahweh, not to us PSALM 115:1   93

O

O Lord heal me; for my bones are vexed Psalm 6:2 12

O Lord, rebuke me not Psalm 6:1 13

On hearing me, people congratulated me, Job 29:11 61

One day when the sons of God Job 1:6 105

One of them, Caiaphas, the high priest John 11:16 107

Open for me the gates of saving justice Psalm 118:19 63

Our Father in heaven Matthew 6:9 14

Our Father which art in heaven Luke 11:2 77

     Matthew 6:9 77

P

Peace I bequeath to you John 14:27 104

R

Rejoice greatly, O daughter of Zion Zechariah 9:9 39

Rejoice with Jerusalem, be glad for her Isaiah 66:10 35

Remove not the ancient landmark Proverbs 22:28 49

Remove not the old landmark Proverbs 23:10 49

Rest in the Lord, and wait patiently for him Psalm 37:7 44

S

Save me God, for the waters have closed Psalm 69:1 10

Seek ye the Lord, all ye meek of the earth Zephaniah 2:3 44

Shout for joy, you heavens; earth exult! Isaiah 49:13 35

T

That is why I am telling you not to worry Matthew 6:25 16

The coming of the kingdom of God Luke 17:20 15

The earth is the Lord's Psalm 24:1 52, 73, 86

The fishers shall also mourn Isaiah 19:8 26

The kingdom of heaven may be compared
   Matthew 13:24 18

The land shall not be sold for ever Leviticus 25:23 58

The Lord is my shepherd Psalm 23:1 33

The Lord Yahweh says this EZEKIEL 47:13   58
The people that walked in darkness ISAIAH 9:2   102
The sower of the good seed MATTHEW 13:37   19
The spirit of Lord Yahweh is on me ISAIAH 61:1   31, 65
The waters will ebb from the sea ISAIAH 19:5   25
The whole wide world will remember PSALM 22:27   115
Then he said to them 'Watch LUKE 12:15   21
Then His Excellency Nehemiah NEHEMIAH 8:9   30
Then the disciples went up to him MATTHEW 13   15
Then the kingdom of heaven will be like this:
    MATTHEW 25:1   20
There was a rich man LUKE 16:19   7
These are Yahweh's orders EXODUS 16:16   48
They will be told they are 'Children ...' HOSEA 2:1   106
This fiftieth year will be a year of jubilee LEVITICUS 25:12   66
Thou didst cause judgement to be heard PSALM 76:8   44
Thou shalt not remove thy neighbours landmark
    DEUTERONOMY 19:14   49
Two men went up to the Temple LUKE 18:10   82

W

We have not listened DANIEL 9:6   75
When I call, answer me God PSALM 4:1   10
When people began being numerous GENESIS 6:1   105
When the righteous are in authority PROVERBS 29:2   31
Wherefore, behold, I send unto you MATTHEW 23:34   119
Who, being in the form of God, PHILIPPIANS 2:6   42

XYZ

Yahweh, hear my voice as I cry PSALM 27:7   89
Yahweh is about to try ISAIAH 3:14   43
Yahweh is merciful and upright PSALM 116:5   94
Yahweh, who can find a home PSALM 15:1   62
Ye shall therefore keep all my statutes LEVITICUS 20:22   47
You will take possession of the country NUMBERS 33:53   47